Interpreting Galatians
for Preaching and Teaching

Kerygma and Church

Interpreting Galatians for Preaching and Teaching

Edited by Scott Nash

Smyth & Helwys Publishing, Inc.©
Macon, Georgia

ISBN 1-880837-87-0

Interpreting Galatians for Preaching and Teaching
Copyright © 1995
Smyth & Helwys Publishing, Inc.

The paper used in this publication meets the minimum requirements of American Standard for Information Sciences—Permanence of paper for Printed Library Materials, ANSI Z39.48–1984.

Library of Congress Cataloging-in-Publication Data

Interpreting Galatians for preaching and teaching/
        edited by Scott Nash.
        x + 182 pp.   6" x 9" (15 x 23 cm.) (Kerygma and church)
        Includes bibliographical references.
        ISBN 1-880837-87-0 (alk. paper)
        1. Bible. N. T. Galatians—Criticism, interpretations, etc.
        2. Bible. N. T. Galatians—Sermons. 3. Sermons, American.
        I. Nash, Robert Scott, 1953–. II. Series.
        BS2685.2.I57   1995
        227'.406—dc20   94-38952
                                                              CIP

Contents

Preface to the Series

Smyth and Helwys Publishing presents the *Kerygma and Church* series in the hope of filling a void in literature available to ministers and churches. In particular, the series seeks to bridge the gulf too often separating the study from the pew and the academic classroom from the context of church life. The series legitimates its existence by the conviction that biblical scholarship has significant and relevant contributions to make to the ongoing life of the community of faith.

Because of its stated aim to connect the serious study of the Bible with the life of the church, the series intends to feature the contributions of persons who themselves are sensitive to the relationship between scholarship and church life. Whether the approach be primarily exegetical or expository, a sensitivity to both endeavors should be evident.

Both academicians and ministers/church leaders will find an avenue here to articulate their understandings of the Kerygma (the church's proclamation). The series further aims to be inclusive of the diversity within the total body of believers. While the series is expressly by Baptists and primarily for Baptists, an inclusive spirit will also at times lead us to consider other perspectives.

As students of Baptist history would expect from any endeavor invoking the revered names of (John) Smyth and (Thomas) Helwys, freedom of inquiry and expression is paramount for this series. A respect for scripture as authoritative religious literature bearing the Kerygma of the Word of God directs scholarship to listen carefully to what is said in order to learn how to respond faithfully. Beyond this healthy concern to "hear and obey," however, no other parameters are permitted to dictate the direction of study or the application of its findings. Through exegesis and exposition of biblical texts, the works of this series will strive to connect the Kerygma of God with the Church of God.

The Editors
Macon, Georgia

Preface

This book bears the task of enabling those who must preach and teach the letter of Paul to the Galatians to preach and teach better than they would have before reading this book. It is a high task both in importance and in ambition. A certain confidence about this particular volume in the Kerygma and Church series guides me to believe that the task has been accomplished. Such is not to say that the present work could not have been even better; of course, it could have been—what book couldn't have been—better! But herein lies a rich wealth of insight about Galatians and its significant message, enough to keep the mental juices flowing for the reader for a long time. Finishing this book will, I hope, not only result in the reader being better prepared to preach and teach Galatians, but will also lead the reader back again and again to Paul's great letter to look for even more insight and inspiration.

The first time I seriously considered the message of Paul's letter to the Galatians, I was a college student recently called to be assistant pastor of my home church in Frankfort, Kentucky. Galatians was the book for the annual winter Bible study. The pastor, Allen Harrod, mined sparkling gems from the epistle's pages and stimulated my inclination to go digging myself. While our quests for truth and faithfulness to Scripture have led us, like Barnabas and Paul, down different paths theologically and denominationally, I remain grateful for his introducing me to the serious study of the Bible.

I am grateful also to each of those professors and pastors who allowed his or her material to be published here. The breadth of perspectives and depth of insights reflected in their words in themselves add both legitimacy and meaning to a book like this. A special word of thanks is extended to Marion Soards for granting permission to include material that I heard him present at the Furman Pastors School. Marty's scholarship is impeccable, and his skill in communicating his thoughts to any audience makes his work ideal for this series.

Essential assistance for this project came, as it does daily, from Jackie Riley and Nancy Hollomon, book editors at Smyth & Helwys. My wife, Dawn, also contributed her excellent typing skills and her gentle prodding with her periodic "When will *your* book be ready?"

During the course of finishing this book I had to finish my time as pastor of the College Hill Baptist Church, Mount Vernon, Georgia. Leaving was postponed beyond what we all knew was best for the church and for the sanity of a long-distance pastor and family purely because of the strong bonds life in that wonderful fellowship had forged. Those who know this unique church also know what I mean. To find in rural South Georgia a church so freed from the bonds of sexism, racism, and traditionalism is to find support for believing that Paul's words really can be true:

There is neither Jew nor Greek, there is neither slave nor free, there is neither male nor female; for you are all one in Christ Jesus. (Gal 3:28)

Scott Nash
Macon, Georgia

Introduction to Teaching the Epistle to the Galatians*

Marion L. Soards

Paul: The Man, the Message, and the Mission**

Through the course of nearly two thousand years of Christian history, probably no person has been more generally loved, hated, and misunderstood than the apostle Paul. Indeed, it is fair to say that the vast majority of those who love and who hate Paul are the ones who least understand him. Thus, we must ask, Who was Paul?

Basically, Paul was a first-century Diaspora (non-Palestinian) Jew who was changed radically from being a violent persecutor of the earliest church to become perhaps the most important missionary in all of Christian history. We know of him and about him from his letters (of the thirteen writings attributed to Paul in the New Testament, Romans, 1 Corinthians, 2 Corinthians, Galatians, Philippians, 1 Thessalonians, and Philemon are almost universally accepted as authentic; whereas Ephesians, Colossians, 2 Thessalonians, 1 Timothy, 2 Timothy, and Titus are the subject of debate about authorship), Acts, and references in other, non-biblical early Christian writings.

In the evidence available from Paul himself, the indication is clear that the apostle was deeply influenced by the cultural streams

---

* In writing about Galatians I am always in the debt of J. Louis Martyn, whose forthcoming Anchor Bible commentary on Galatians will be a milestone in Pauline studies. Thanks, Lou.

** See my earlier work, *The Apostle Paul: An Introduction to His Writings and Teaching* (New York: Paulist, 1987), for a fuller discussion of many of the following items.

of both Judaism and Hellenism (the Greek way of life that had spread and dominated the Mediterranean world since the time of Alexander the Great). Paul's strong background in Judaism is evident in (a) his being a zealous Pharisee (Phil 3:5-6); (b) his being schooled in rabbinic tradition, as seen in his language (1 Cor 15:3); (c) his use of the Old Testament as his Bible, an authoritative source (Gal 3:10); (d) his doing of midrashic exegesis (Galatians 3 and 1 Corinthians 10); and (e) his clear, nearly constant concern for the Law (Galatians 3-4 and Romans 7).

[As an important aside for understanding Paul, especially as he wrote Galatians, we must recognize that for first-century Judaism the Law was not what Christians once thought it to be. The Law functioned in the broad pattern of Jewish religion that was founded on the twin pillars of *election* and *atonement*. First-century Judaism *began* with the recognition that God chose Israel to be God's people. In relation to this election, God gave the Law to Israel as the norm for life as the people of God. Israel kept the Law as a divinely designed response to election. Thus, the Law was a means of participating in election; it was not a means to achieve salvation. Jews did not keep the Law in order to earn merit so as to win salvation. Judaism taught that God chose Israel and gave the Law as the norm for life in response to God's election. *Keeping the Law was Israel's side of the covenant that God made with the nation.* Moreover, for those who violated or failed to keep the Law, Judaism trusted in God's provisions for atonement. If a person out of keeping with the standards of the covenant (the Law) repented and performed appropriate acts of contrition (alms, sacrifices, etc.), Judaism taught that God promised forgiveness.]

Paul also demonstrated a thoroughgoing background in *Greco-Roman Hellenism*. According to Acts he was a citizen of Tarsus. Quite clearly he had been educated in the Greek fashion as is seen in his very practice of reading and writing (Jews in this period taught and recited orally), his use of the logic of popular Greek philosophy (Rom 3:1; 6:1), and his comfort with images and illustrations from Greco-Roman thought and life: athletics (1 Cor 9:24-27), military (1 Thess 5:8), dress (1 Thess 2:5), and child-rearing (1 Thess 2:7, 11). Moreover, while Paul turned to the Old Testament as authoritative scripture, he used the Septuagint, the Greek translation of the Hebrew scriptures; and he was at home interpreting scripture allegorically in the fashion of Greek, not rabbinic, exposition (Galatians 4). Finally, he always referred to himself as Paul, not Saul, in his writings. We know his more Jewish name, Saul, from Acts.

Interpreters once set these two seemingly contradictory backgrounds against each other, arguing that valid comprehension of Paul and his teaching required selecting the most vital framework. Yet, now we know that such juxtaposition is false and simplistic, for in the centuries prior to the time of Paul, Judaism and Hellenism had come into a powerful confrontation and relationship that deeply affected Judaism and yielded a distinctive view of the world.

The meeting point of these once distinct backgrounds was evident in the outlook of *apocalyptic eschatology*. This mind-set was a form of Jewish temporal dualism (Gal 1:4; 2 Cor 5:17) that looked for imminent future judgment—wrath, salvation, death, life, the day of the Lord—and lived with a essential belief that humanity lived on the boundary of two worlds: one dying and one being born (1 Cor 10:11). People with such a worldview typically understood that their own generation was the last (1 Thess 4:17), so they had a sense of special urgency about life (1 Cor 7:29-31). Careful study of Paul's epistles shows that apocalyptic eschatology characterizes the apostle's thinking and teaching.

Yet, we should see that Paul's Christian apocalyptic eschatological worldview was a modification of typical Jewish apocalyptic eschatological thinking. Jewish apocalyptic thought held that there are two ages, *the present evil age* and *the age to come*. The present evil age is the world in which humans currently live; the age to come is a supernatural realm of the power of God. There is no continuity between these ages. Apocalyptic Jewish eschatology believed that at some future moment God would break into the human world and bring the age to come. When God intervened in the present evil age, the age to come would be established as a new reality, ordained and directed by God, and the present evil age would pass away. The age to come was the hope of those who lived in the present evil age, experiencing oppression by the forces of evil. One may diagram such a worldview in the following way:

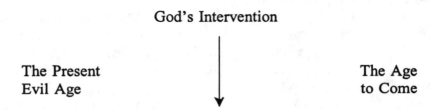

Paul's letters, however, present a modified Christian apocalyptic eschatology. For the apostle the first temporal era is "the present evil age" (Gal 1:4; 1 Cor 2:6-8). This age is ruled by the god of this world (2 Cor 4:4), Satan, and by the elemental spirits of the universe (Gal 4:3; 1 Cor 2:8). Under the influence of these rulers, this age is at strong odds with God (1 Cor 15:24-28; Rom 8:37-39). Nevertheless, this age is passing away (1 Cor 7:31). In turn, the second temporal era is called "a new creation" (Gal 6:15; 2 Cor 5:17). This new age comes as God *in Christ* defeats the forces in opposition to him (Gal 6:14; 1 Cor 7:31; Rom 5:21), and it is established as the age of divine glory (1 Thess 2:10-12; 1 Cor 15:20-28; 2 Cor 4:17; Rom 5:2, 21). For Paul, *the present exists as the juncture of the ages* or as a mingling of the ages (1 Cor 10:11; 2 Cor 5:16).

Here 1 Cor 10:11 is crucial. In this verse Paul described himself and other humans as those "on whom the ends of the ages have come." Many modern translations obscure Paul's idea in this line, translating it "on whom the end of the ages has come." This rendering implies that Paul stood at the end of time and looked back at the ages (dispensations?) that had gone before—but, he did not. The phrase literally says, "upon whom the ends of the ages have met." In other words, Paul perceived that he and other humans lived at the overlapping of two distinct times. This meeting of the ages had come about as a result of the cross of Christ (1 Cor 1:17-18) and it will conclude, marking the absolute end of the present evil age, at the coming of Christ from heaven (1 Thess 2:19; 3:13; 4:13-18; 1 Cor 15:23-28). To diagram Paul's Christian apocalyptic eschatological worldview:

God's Intervention in—

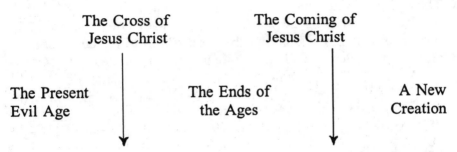

| The Cross of | | The Coming of | |
| Jesus Christ | | Jesus Christ | |

| The Present | The Ends of | A New |
| Evil Age | the Ages | Creation |

Paul was called, he worked, he thought, and he taught others that they lived in this mixed time between the cross and the coming of Jesus Christ. *Already* the old world was passing away, and *already* the new was present; but *not yet* had evil been eliminated, and *not yet* had God's reign been established. Paul lived with faith in the cross of Christ and with hope in Christ's coming.

Paul and the Galatians

In the original sense of the designation, *Galatia* was a territory in northern Asia Minor. Originally the region was populated by Celts who migrated there from Gaul in the first half of the third century B.C.E. In Greek, *galatai* (Galatians) is a variant of *keltai* (Celts). In 25 B.C.E. the last of the Galatian kings died, leaving his kingdom in the hands of the Romans, who reorganized the area into a province by adding other districts (Isauria, parts of Lycaonia, Paphlagonia, Pisidia, Phrygia, and Pontus) to Galatia. But, the province as a whole bore no official name; rather, it went by the names of its parts.

Paul's Relationship to the Galatians

Paul himself wrote of his original dealings with the Galatians saying, "You know it was because of an illness of the flesh that I preached the gospel to you at first." He continued, "You would have plucked out your eyes and given them to me—if possible." These lines and the mention of the "large letters" of Paul's handwriting (6:11) lead some interpreters to conclude Paul had problems with his vision and this forced him to reside among the Galatians. Perhaps this is true, though one cannot say with certainty. We do, however, know that Paul traveled in Galatia more than once, although from the account in Acts 16-19 we know few details of his trips. Nevertheless, the reader of Galatians may infer that Paul's first contact with the Galatians was in a time of personal crisis.

The Problem That Elicited This Letter

According to Gal 1:6, Paul wrote to the Galatians because they were deserting their calling by his preaching and turning to what he caustically called a "different gospel." This other gospel was proclaimed among the Galatians by a group of outsiders who came among them after Paul's departure and who were probably in their midst when Paul wrote. Paul asserted the Galatians were "foolish . . . bewitched" (3:1). They had moved from their Christian origin in the Spirit to the realm of the Flesh. Indeed, Paul suggested that the Galatians were seeking to receive the Spirit out of *the workings of the Law* rather than out of *the hearing of Faith*. In other words, under the influence of those who had come among them, the

Galatians were moving toward Law-observance. This is clear from the references in 4:10 to the calendar, in 5:2 to circumcision, and in 5:3 to the "whole Law."

Those Whom Paul Opposed in Galatians

In order to understand what Paul is saying in Galatians, it is necessary to gain some idea of who the outsiders who had come among the Galatians were and what they had said that had caused the problem. To do this one must engage in a "mirror-reading" of the text, that is, the problem in Galatia and those whom Paul opposed must be reconstructed from Paul's descriptions and statements in the letter itself. This is somewhat similar to listening to someone talking on the telephone. From what is said on one end of the line, an attentive listener may be able to infer what was said by the other partner in the conversation. This involves speculation, so that there are risks that the "other" side of the conversation may be misunderstood or distorted; but without this reconstruction, Paul's statements are completely incomprehensible. Thus, one must run the risks of reconstruction, but only with extreme caution.

Paul recorded three relatively neutral pieces of information about those who came among the Galatians after his departure. Of them he wrote:

> (1) They preached "another gospel," different from that preached in Galatia by Paul; he said it was a perversion of the gospel (1:6-7). This is Paul's description, however; and an unbiased reader of the letter should infer that in the minds of these preachers, the gospel they proclaimed was *the* gospel, not a perversion.

> (2) They "troubled" the Galatians (1:7). The message of these preachers disturbed or frightened the Galatians; it "upset" them (5:12).

(3) The preachers in Galatia were circumcised (6:13).

These statements serve as fixed points in the effort to imagine those whom Paul opposed in Galatia. Using other information in the letter, one may draw between the points to develop a fuller picture. Doing so, it seems that after Paul departed from Galatia some evangelists came there independently preaching a message— enough like Paul's to be regarded as "the gospel," but sufficiently different for Paul to call it a perversion or "another gospel." This new preaching stirred up the Galatians. Paul seems to have associated these people with the "false believers" of the Jerusalem Conference (2:4). This inference makes sense, for the preachers clearly advocated observance of the Law by Christians. Moreover, in addition to preaching a gospel different from that proclaimed by Paul, Gal 1:10 suggests these evangelists had accused Paul of being a *people-pleaser*, a preacher of a watered-down gospel.

In fairness to these evangelists, they probably understood themselves to be Christian Jews engaged in a Law-observant mission to the Gentiles, not primarily Paul's opponents. They do appear to have criticized Paul for preaching a Law-free gospel, but it was the apostle who cast them into the role of adversaries, not they. Thus, the major task at this point is to discern what these people considered the "good news" to be.

The Theology of Paul's Opponents

From Paul's letter, one learns something of the content of the Galatian preachers' proclamation:

(1) The Law was their point of departure and the heart of their theology (5:1-4). They probably spoke of "the Law of Christ" (6:2)—for this is not a Pauline phrase. They probably taught that God's Law was affirmed and interpreted by God's Messiah, so that Jesus was the Messiah of the Law. Their theology had *an additive pattern*: They viewed the

Law as primary and *added* Christ to it as the authoritative interpreter. They probably taught that to obey the Law as interpreted by Christ was to become "Abraham's off-springs" (3:6-18).

(2) The "good news" is *news* and *good* for the Gentiles. This is obvious since the preachers were in Galatia, advocating the Law among Gentiles. They argued that the Law, formerly given to Israel alone, had become available to Gentiles through the interpretation of the Messiah. The preachers themselves were probably not meticulous in their observance of the Law (6:13). They appear to have understood the Law—as they said it was interpreted by the Messiah—to be a reduction of the former, more stringent requirements. They focused on the overt portions of the Law (circumcision and calendar) so that the Law had come to be for all. Moreover, they did not see the problem Paul recognized, namely, the conflict between Christ and the Law. Instead, they thought of Law-observance as an obligatory sign, as the manageable human end of a covenant with God.

(3) Clearly the preachers in Galatia used the Old Testament as a textual tool in dissemination of their religious propaganda. They probably understood the Old Testament as ritual prescription and believed and taught that proper observance of the prescription assured one of receiving the Spirit (see 3:2-3). Throughout Galatians one sees Paul take up certain of their favorite texts and engage himself in rather original exegesis. What is remarkable is that Paul and the preachers *agreed* that proper interpretation of the Old Testament provides truth and is essential.

(4) The "good news" proclaimed by the preachers was conditional. At 4:17 Paul employed the image of the gate

and gatekeepers. The preachers at Galatia had threatened to shut the Galatians out if they failed to comply with the admonition to Law-observance. The preachers must have understood the Law as the narrow gate to salvation and themselves as the gatekeepers who guarded the way of righteousness.

(5) The preachers appear to have taught that the "key" to the gate was Law-observance (4:17), especially circumcision (5:2, 13).

Paul's Advice to the Galatians

Paul insisted that the gospel he preached among the Galatians is the only gospel. Anything else, no matter what it is called or who preaches it, is a perversion. Paul stated boldly that his apostolic commission and the origin of his message were the results of divine revelation. He did not learn his message from any human. In contrast, he suggested the preachers in Galatia were concerned only with "the flesh." This mistaken concern was seen in their focus on keeping the Law, especially in their concern with circumcision. They were bound up with human activity in the present evil age, *not* with the Spirit who is known and experienced by the power of God—the same power that raised Jesus from the dead.

One of the main lines of Paul's argument in Galatians is his juxtaposition of Faith and the Law. This contrast reflects Paul's apocalyptic mind-set, for he thought of Faith and the Law as elements in two opposing realms, one potent and the other impotent (3:21). One sees this at Gal 2:16 where Paul spoke of "the faith of Christ" and "the workings of the Law." Literally, his phrases in Greek say, "out of the faith of Christ" and "out of the workings of the Law." He was thinking here of two realms "out of" which powerful results emanate.

For Paul these words (along with others like Spirit and Flesh) functioned as technical terms that describe two opposing realms, one God's and the other in opposition to God. They are cosmic in scope, and humans are in either one realm or the other. Persons in God's realm are being saved, whereas those in the other realm are lost, cursed. Accordingly, those "in Faith" are saved and those "under the Law" are cursed, for Jesus Christ rescued those "in Faith" whereas those "under the Law" are caught up in the Law's impotence and are trapped.

The good news for those under the Law is that Jesus Christ gave himself, invading the realm of the Law and becoming cursed as he died crucified. And then, God revealed his power, overcame the curse, and saved humanity by raising Jesus from the dead. Moreover, from "the faith of Christ" comes *Faith itself* (5:22), by which humans, like Abraham, are set right with God. Contrary to the claim of the preachers in Galatia, salvation is not tied to human actions (the workings of the Law). For saving Faith is not a human product; it is a fruit of the Spirit (5:22), a gracious gift from God. In contrast, from "the workings of the Law," the system of righteousness-maintenance advocated by the preachers, comes "the curse of the Law" (3:13) whereby all things are "consigned to/under sin" (3:22).

At Gal 3:15-18 Paul showed the ridiculousness of the additive pattern (Law + Christ = new Law) advocated by the preachers in Galatia. He said that attempts to add Christ to the Law showed ignorance of the priority of God's promise to Abraham. One cannot add Christ to the Law because the promise and its fulfillment stand above the Law and coexist apart from the existence of the Law.

God's Promise to Abraham	- - - - - - - - - → [the Law]	The Fulfillment of the Promise in Christ

Theological Keys to Galatians

Paul perceived that salvation comes through the power of God: Paul was called by this power; Jesus Christ was raised by it; and the Galatians had Faith because of God's power.

From this starting point Paul saw that the Galatians had made a dangerous mistake in turning to the Law, for humans are cursed by the workings of the Law. Since salvation is based in God's promise to Abraham and the fulfillment of the promise in Jesus Christ, the Law has nothing to do with the promise. In Christ, the fulfillment of the promise, God acted to save humanity from its involvement with the impotent, "elemental spirits of the universe," one of which was the Law. Christ himself became cursed by the Law. Nevertheless, God raised Jesus from the dead and thereby demonstrated his power, that Jesus Christ is his Son, and that the Law is impotent.

Paul's message to the Galatians was that involvement with the Law is enslavement to the Flesh. He called for the Galatians to abandon the error of their ways and to stand fast "in Christ" (not "under the Law"), for Jesus Christ, and he alone, means freedom (5:1).

Commentary

Galatians 1:1–2:21

Here Paul opened the letter, getting right to the problem as he moved to defend his apostleship, which was under attack. Remarkably, he did not argue about his apostleship out of pride, but rather as a defense for the gospel he preached, which was the motivation for his apostolic work.

The opening (1:1-5). Paul identified himself as a "apostle," a noun formed from the Greek verb *apostellein*, which means "to send." In other words, Paul was one who was sent by God. Paul aimed, even in this opening, to establish his independence from other human agents. His declaration, however, immediately raises a question: If Paul was not brought to Christ by a human agent of God, then how was it that he became a Christian and an apostle? Paul stated directly that it was by the same power of God that raised Jesus Christ from the dead. With his starting point set, Paul spoke of "grace and peace" to the churches in Galatia. These words were a relatively standard greeting from the apostle to the congregations to which he wrote. Commentators suggest that "grace" is the work of God among humanity, whereas "peace" is the result of God's working.

One should notice at the outset of this letter that Paul's perspective and remarks are profoundly theological. Paul's *christology* is evident in his understanding that Jesus is both the Messiah and the Lord. Paul's *soteriology* comes through as he referred to the Lord Jesus Christ's having given himself for the sins of humans in order to deliver them. Paul's *eschatological worldview* is clear from the mention of "the present evil age," and the thoroughly *theological cast* of Paul's thinking is seen as he explained that the saving work of Christ occurred "according to the will of God." Thus, from the outset of the letter, in these brief lines we see Paul's christologically focused apocalyptic eschatological theological perspective. Everything he thought and said in the rest of the letter finds its meaning in that context.

Paul's objection to the situation, or the problem in Galatia (1:6-9). The Galatians were turning away from the gospel Paul preached to a different gospel. We should notice that according to Paul the Galatians were turning (a) from the "grace" of Christ and (b) from "the one who called" them, that is, God. Yet, Paul insisted there is no other gospel than the one he proclaimed in Galatia; there is otherwise only perversion! Moreover, Paul reported that this turning on the part of the Galatians occurred at the instigation of some troublesome preachers. From Paul's comments throughout the letter we find a Jewish cast to the concerns and activities of these preachers—at 4:10 we find they focused on calendar; at 5:2-3 we find they emphasized circumcision and the Law; at 6:13 we learn that they were circumcised. Yet, these were not Jewish missionaries who were simply trying to convert Christians to Judaism. Both they and Paul referred to their message as the *gospel*, albeit a different gospel, so that we should understand the preachers to have been Christian Jews. Paul said, "Let them be *anathema*, that is literally, "Let them be accursed to the infernal region"; so that any good Greek-speaker would get Paul's rude point: He meant "to hell with them!"

Paul's retort (1:10). Paul's question here reflects what the newly-come preachers said about him, namely, he was just a "people-pleaser." Apparently when the preachers were asked to explain the difference between their message and Paul's they suggested that Paul watered-down the message, not including proclamation about Law-observance, so that his message was not as demanding as theirs. Yet, now, Paul's boldness shows a disregard for all others but God. The phrasing of the second part of Gal 1:10 is telling, "If I were still pleasing people, I wouldn't be a servant of Christ." When Paul spoke of "still pleasing people," he must have meant to refer to his past life in Judaism, to his former involvement with the Law and his previous passion for Law-observance. Thus, according to Paul, preaching about the Law was itself pleasing people as one offered legal norms that brought a sense of security to those who observed the Law.

People do like rules and guidelines. Living by the rule book is secure. There is no dynamic tension, no gray. Rules-for-living even allow a smug self-confidence as people are sure they are in the right.

Reiteration and clarification of Paul's objection (1:11-12).
From his strenuous protest in Gal 1:10, Paul moved briefly to explicate his assessment of what was happening in Galatia. Paul's gospel was good news, and the primary reason it was *really* good was that the news was not a message that came from humanity. Paul's statement is rich. He did not take an anthropological starting point in his ministry, for the good news he preached did not come to him from a human, nor was it taught to him by a human. Paul's gospel came *by revelation of Jesus Christ.* This remark could mean either (a) that Jesus was the agent of a communication of some content to Paul or (b) that the encounter of Paul with the risen Lord Jesus Christ itself implied the content of the gospel he preached. The latter interpretation is more likely grammatically and in terms of the plain sense of Paul's other statements throughout Galatians.

Yet, all this makes one wonder, Was Paul lying; was he mad; or, was he telling the truth? Paul actually seems to have anticipated such questions about what he claimed, for at Gal 1:20 he wrote, "What I write you, before God, 'I do not lie!' "

Paul's past, his calling, and his early work (1:13-24). This section of the epistle, retrospective as it is, picks up the thought from Gal 1:10 concerning Paul's "still pleasing people." From beginning to end here Paul was illustrating his independence in order to show the error of the Galatians' tendency toward taking up Law-observance.

Paul told of his past in Judaism. He had been a zealous, contented, well-placed Jew. He had devoted himself with remarkable enthusiasm to the "traditions of the elders," that is, to the Law and its careful interpretation and to obedience to the Law. Yet, Paul recalled his *call.* As Paul has told the story, the reader learns that Paul experienced an act of divine intervention; and that interruption by God came according to God's own preordained will. Paul was called, according to God's eternal will that had preceded even his birth, in order that God might make him and send him to be an apostle to the Gentiles. It is striking to compare Paul's words with those of the prophet Jeremiah as that prophet recounted his own call by God:

Paul: God had set me apart from my mother's womb, and had called me through his grace; [God] was pleased to reveal his Son to me, in order that I might preach him among the Gentiles [or, literally, "the nations"].

Jeremiah: Now the word of the Lord came to me saying, "Before I formed you in the womb I knew you, and before you were born I consecrated you; I appointed you a prophet to the nations!" (Jer 1:4-5)

Thus, in reporting his call by divine intervention, Paul paraphrased the lines of the call of Jeremiah to establish his independence and to document his direct call by God. The one truly new element in Paul's report is the reference to God's Son, so that we see christology at the forefront of Paul's theological reflection.

Paul recounted, moreover, his early work in order to corroborate further his independence from other human agents. He reported that at the outset of his work he was barely known to the apostles and to those in Jerusalem. His point is clear, namely, that he was not sent out from or by humans; rather, Paul was sent from and by God. Thus, in what he said and did, he was concerned to do God's pleasure, not the pleasure of human beings.

Paul at Jerusalem (2:1-10). Scholars debate exactly what and when the incident reported here took place. F. F. Bruce contended that Paul was referring to the events that are reported at Acts 11:30. Bo Reicke argued that Paul has the incident from Acts 18:22 in mind. The majority or consensus of New Testament interpreters, however, relates the remarks here to the events that are reported in Acts 15, the so-called Apostolic Council in Jerusalem. If there is a chronological difficulty with this correlation, scholars judge that

Luke (in Acts) was not clear or precise about the exact sequence of events in the life of the early church.

Although Paul was adamant about his independence and explained that early in his ministry he had only minimal relations to the church in Jerusalem and to its leaders, he recalled here that later in his ministry he did have dealings with Jerusalem; but even then he said that he had moved as a result of divine revelation, not in accordance with human volition. Verse 2 presents a problem. What was Paul doing? From what he said earlier and later in this letter we should see that he did not go to Jerusalem to seek an endorsement from the church there; rather, when he went to Jerusalem he acted in order to assure the unity of the various portions of the early church.

Verse 3 scores a major point in Paul's argument against the Galatians being concerned with observance of the Law: Titus, a Gentile like the Galatians, had accompanied Paul on the trip to Jerusalem, and he was not required by the Jerusalem leaders to be circumcised. Indeed, at Jerusalem when the "false believers" tried to impose the observance of the Law on the mission to the Gentiles, they failed. They did not gain support from the Jerusalem leaders, who embraced the Law-free mission to the Gentiles in warm fellowship. Thus, at Jerusalem there was a recognition of the different but equal, complementary missions to the Jews, on the one hand, and to the Gentiles, on the other. Unfortunately, with the passage of a short span of time, these different but equal and complementary missions became separate-but-equal. At the meeting in Jerusalem all present did not have the foresight to ask about Jewish and Gentile Christians *together*, so a serious problem arose later in Antioch.

In a closing note to this memory, Paul recollected only that at Jerusalem there had been a request that he should remember the "poor." In other words, the leaders of the church in Jerusalem asked Paul to work among his Gentile converts to bring some assistance to the Jerusalem Christians. Members of that church had fallen on hard times in the mid-first century because after pooling all their material resources, they had exhausted their goods in the course of caring for those who were needy in a difficult period of famine that struck Palestine. Having practiced charity, the Jerusalem Christians were in need of charity; and Paul reported he was eager to help.

Paul versus Cephas at Antioch (2:11-14). Scholarly debate on these verses runs from the esoteric (Is this Cephas really Simon Peter?) to the obvious (What was the problem?). The verses bring us to the early church's confrontation with the issue that had been avoided at the Jerusalem conference, namely, what should be done about Law observance when Jews and Gentiles who are Christians come together. The key to the crisis in Antioch was that the problem arose over table-fellowship, the very place where Christians came together to eat and to celebrate the Lord's Supper. In the debate we see that Peter (Cephas) and those who took his side chose to favor a pre-Christian Jewish tradition that labored to preserve Jewish food purity regulations in the context of a gathering of Jewish and Gentile Christians. Peter and his companions withdrew from table-fellowship with Gentile Christians. Paul on the other hand, and whoever agreed with him, chose to embody the mentality of Christian unity that is declared dramatically in Gal 3:28, "In Christ there is no Jew or Greek!" This absolute valuing of unity, despite differences in sensibilities over the Law, was a bold declaration of the new reconciliation that had been won in Christ.

From Paul's perspective, Peter's maintaining distance from the Gentiles (or the insistence of some others that Gentiles comply with Jewish food codes) set the Law over Christ. Thus, Peter and the others with (or near) him gave the Law the upper hand in an effort to regulate the unity of Jews and Gentiles in the context of Christ. For Paul, an insistence on Law-observance attempted to maintain the structures of the age before Christ rather than yield to and celebrate new patterns of relations that are created in the context of the new creation that Christ accomplished.

Paul's explication of his position (2:15-21). This is one of the most difficult passage in all of Paul's epistles. It presents problems for translation and, in turn, for interpretation. Commentators disagree sharply about what Paul was saying here, and all who study the passage admit its ambiguity.

An interpretive key is found in noticing that Paul's word "justify" comes from the Greek verb *dikaioun*, which means "set right," a concept that carries over into English in the notion of margin justification in typing and printing. Here, however, one should note that the verb is *passive*, so that Paul's concern was with *being justified* or, literally, "to be set right." The question Paul addressed in these lines is this: "What sets human beings right with God?" In this discussion Paul staked out two options: Humans are either set right with God by *the workings of the Law*, or humans are set right by *the hearing of Faith*.

The juxtaposition of Law and Faith in relationship to the question of how humans are set right with God is striking. On the one hand, as we noted above in the introduction to Galatians, the Law was thought to have a particular function in Judaism: Israel was elected by God's gracious choice and was given the Law as a normative response for the maintenance of the relationship God had brought into being through grace. On the other hand, Faith is a peculiarly important, but difficult Pauline idea. At Gal 2:16 Paul said, "A human is not justified out the workings of the Law, but only through the faith of Jesus Christ." At Gal 3:23 Paul said that "Faith came"; and at 5:22 Paul declared that Faith is "fruit of the Spirit." Bluntly and somewhat simply stated, for Paul the Law is something humans do and Faith is something that God creates in humans through the saving work of Jesus Christ's own faithfulness and through the presence and power of the Spirit at work in the world.

In this discussion, Gal 2:17 is notoriously difficult. The RSV translated the line as follows:

But, if in our endeavor to be justified in Christ, we ourselves were found to be sinners, is Christ then an agent of sin? Certainly not!

The NRSV reads similarly,

But if, in our effort to be justified in Christ, we ourselves have been found to be sinners, is Christ then a servant of sin? Certainly not!

The NIV translates the verse this way:

If, while we seek to be justified in Christ, it becomes evident that we ourselves are sinners, does that mean that Christ promotes sin? Absolutely not!

It is possible, even preferable, however, to read the verse in the following manner:

But, if we are found seeking to be justified in Christ, indeed we ourselves are sinners; then, is Christ a minister of sin? May it never be!

Confirmation for this understanding comes in the parallel statement that follows in Gal 2:18, "But if I build up again those things which I tore down, then I prove myself a transgressor"; and in the bold declaration of Gal 2:21, "I do not nullify the grace of God; for if justification were through the Law, then Christ died for nothing."

A summary of Paul's line of thought in Gal 2:15-21 runs as follows: The Galatians, who were Gentiles, were moving toward Law-observance as a way of maintaining their good-standing with God. To discourage them, Paul said that he and his companions, Jews, who once did observe the Law, now knew that no one is set right or stays right with God by Law-observance. People are only right with God—set right and stay right—by virtue of what God did in the cross of Jesus Christ and by what God does through the

Holy Spirit. If this is not true, Christ died for nothing. If people who hear the gospel and believe subsequently seek to maintain their relationship to God by Law-observance, they deny God's grace and back away from their calling in and by Faith. People relate to God because Christ is alive in them, not by what they do and do not accomplish themselves. Moreover, Paul saw the Law as a trap, for it is impotent to do what those seeking to relate to God through Law-observance hope it will do for them. But, Paul said, Christ is not powerless! In Christ and with Christ in us, humans are set right with God.

At this juncture, Paul's argumentation had taken him to a strange point. Thus, in the next section of the letter the apostle had to argue carefully and persuasively that he was correct. Thus, in what follows, we shall follow Paul through a series of complex exegetical and logical explanations that seek to validate his position.

Galatians 3:1–5:12

In the second major section of the letter Paul engaged in exegesis as he worked to establish that the Christian—Gentile or Jew—is free from any obligation to observe the Law. Paul's arguments are subtle, cast in ancient forms of rhetoric that are unfamiliar, and so, often difficult for modern readers. Paul's exegesis is quite original, again cast in ancient forms that are difficult, that even seem strained—but the forms and logic would have been very impressive to an ancient audience that shared Paul's rhetorical assumptions and standards.

Paul confronts the Galatians (3:1-5). Paul debated sarcastically and ironically with the apparent contention of the Galatians that they would profit from observance of the Law. He asked a series of rhetorical questions to which the answers should be obvious, although apparently they were not in Galatia. The basic issue is this: How did the Galatians receive the Spirit? Paul presented two options. They either received the Spirit *out of the workings of the Law* or *out of the hearing of Faith.*

It is instructive to notice here that Paul juxtaposed, first, Law and Faith and, then, Spirit and Flesh; in turn, he created rhetorical parallels between, first, Spirit and Faith and, then, Flesh and Law. As Paul created these pairs of opposites and equals he made an important point: The Spirit comes only by the hearing of Faith. As the Spirit bears fruit and Faith comes into the world by the work of God in Jesus Christ, humans believe in the gospel and the Spirit takes hold in their lives and brings them into a new powerful and creative relationship with God. Moreover, it is helpful throughout Galatians to notice the way Paul coupled and set pairs of words in relation to one another. These sets of words, particularly the pairs of opposites, reflect Paul's apocalyptically structured eschatological mind. The apostle saw God at work overcoming the structures of the past and creating the dynamic structures of God's future.

Paul's first exegetical argument (3:6-9). In order to prove his point about the needlessness of Law-observance among the Galatians Paul launched an exegetical argument. The form is midrashic, that is, Paul creatively retold a well-known episode from the Old Testament and applied the story to the contemporary situation he faced so that the original story provided guidance and insight for those whom Paul himself addressed. This midrashic exposition treats the Abraham story, which was a favorite portion of the Old Testament for Jews to use with Gentiles as they sought to make proselytes from among the Gentiles. Abraham was the *first* Jew, himself a convert from a pagan background. Paul's point in this discussion for the sake of the Galatians comes in Gal 3:7, "Thus you know that the ones out of Faith, these are the children of Abraham." The Law is nowhere in sight and apparently irrelevant for the life of persons called through Faith to a new relationship to God.

Another exegetical argument (3:10-14). Again, Paul offered a midrashic argument. He still sharply contrasted or juxtaposed Law and Faith. But, now the apostle elaborated his thinking: The Law curses while Faith blesses. Indeed, Christ himself, the bearer of Faith into the world as the agent of the fruit-Faith-bearing Spirit, was cursed by the Law in order to redeem humanity from the curse of the Law.

We should notice in this argument that Paul understood in Gal 3:14 that the Gentiles had entered into the realm of God's power and grace. This idea may seem odd, but the Septuagintal quotation in Gal 3:8 that mentions "the nations" (in some translations) uses the same Greek word that here is usually translated "Gentiles." Paul was arguing that God's action in Christ was *the* realization of God's promise that was made to Abraham. Moreover, the *clear* (and in Galatia, *experienced*) sign of the actualization of God's promise is that Jews and Gentiles alike receive the Spirit through Faith (not the Law).

Paul clarified his argument through illustration (3:15-18). To make sure his point was understood and to drive it home to his audience in Galatia, Paul argued by analogy to a legal matter, *a will*. This is still more imaginative exposition, although perhaps not strictly midrash. Paul's logic, although related to Roman law, is quite clear: A will stands; anyone other than the one who makes the will cannot amend it once it has been set; and a will is intended to be (necessarily) fulfilled.

Thus, Paul argued that God's promise to Abraham is really like a will. First, *there are terms to the will*; it is set for "Abraham and his offspring [seed]." The word for "offspring" or "seed" in Greek is *sperma*, a collective noun that functions exactly in Greek the way the word "seed" functions in English. One buys five pounds of *seed* at a store. This does not mean that a single seed weighs five pounds, rather one purchases a mass of seeds that weigh five pounds. It is possible in Greek, as in English, to refer to the plural "seeds" (*spermata* in Greek). Paul made a significant point from the use of the singular *sperma* ("seed") rather than the plural *spermata* ("seeds") in the Septuagint. He worked off the singular form to argue that God's promise was *not* given to Abraham and all those who are Law-observant ("seeds"); God made a promise only to Abraham and one other (his "seed"), namely, Jesus Christ.

Second, *there is no amending God's promise!* The Law (and Law-observance) came 430 years after the promise of God to Abraham. Therefore, the Law cannot amend the promise of God to Abraham and his "seed." *But,* one thinks and objects immediately, cannot God who issued the promise (as if it were a will) amend the promise, if God is so pleased? This is a crucial question, and Paul is one step ahead of this query that is potentially damaging to his heated argument.

Paul's reply to the objection (3:19-20). Paul declared—imagine a former, zealous Pharisaic Jew saying this—that the very God who made the promise to Abraham did not give the Law to Israel. Rather, angels did. Paul denied the divine origin of the Law!

How did Paul know this astounding piece of information? Clearly there was a Jewish legend current in Paul's time that suggested that angels *delivered* the Law to Moses on Sinai. We see the idea in a variety of places: Here in Galatians; in Acts 7:53; in Josephus, *Jewish Antiquities* 15.136; and perhaps in Deut 33:2 (?). The idea in all other references than this one is that the Law was so weighty that it took a squad of the heavenly host to deliver the information. Thus, God's dignity was preserved by maintaining some distance from direct communication with a human, and the significance of the Law was underscored by its having been given through God's own messengers, the angels.

Moreover, through creative logic Paul put the idea of the angelic deliverance of the Law to a very different use from any of his contemporaries. He argued that the angelic delivery of the Law meant that Moses was a *mediator.* (The same idea and term, "mediator," designates Moses in Heb 9:15.) Paul argued here uniquely that had God, who is one, given the Law, then, God could have done it directly—God's self in direct relationship to the many of Israel—for God is one, not a group in need of a representative. Yet, Moses mediated the Law to Israel; so that he was the representative of one group (the angels) to another group (the people of Israel).

If the Law did not come directly from God, then why was it given? In response to this question we see that even though he argued against God's giving the Law, Paul still maintained a high view of the Law. The angels gave the Law as helpful guidelines, because humans transgressed God's will. The Law was, for Paul as he argued in Galatians, a clear statement—given by the very angels of God—indeed, a valid statement of God's will for humanity, especially Israel.

More from Paul on the Law (3:21-22). While Paul insisted that the Law is not inherently contrary to God's will, nevertheless, he contended that the Law did not come directly from God with God's own power; and so, the Law is impotent. At most, according to Paul, positively the Law revealed the sinfulness of humanity. The Law served to unite humanity in the common condition of sinfulness, so that the promised blessing of God to Abraham could be given *out of Faith*, the faith of Jesus Christ, to all those who believe–to those in the realm of Faith who live by the power of the Spirit.

The end of the Law and the coming of Faith (3:23-29). Paul declared that the Law confined or constrained humanity *until Faith came*, which Faith did in Jesus Christ. The Law was a warden—a pedagogical supervisor or a prison master—that served (literally) *until Christ.* The Law served in this capacity so that humanity "might be justified out of Faith."

But now, Paul insisted, Faith had come, so there was no more need for the former warden. Now *all* are *children* of God through faith in Jesus Christ—Faith that came in Jesus himself and that now takes hold and transforms the lives of humans as God works through the Holy Spirit. All this means that *there is no division in Christ*, be it in terms of ethnicity, social status, or sexual-social roles. Interpreters often suggest that behind Gal 3:28 lay an early Christian confessional formula that expressed the transformation of human existence and the new relationships brought into existence through Jesus Christ. Whether or not that is correct, the sense of Paul's statement epitomizes the meaning of the Christ-event at the level of human life. Christ is the all-embracing cosmic agent of reconciliation, to whom we are all to cling and to whom we are all to conform. Put simply, because of Christ, we see that in Christ human distinctions do not matter before God. The Lordship of Christ is a reality that we are called to obey and experience. God's new creation in Christ does not depend upon our affirmation for it to be real; rather, we are called by grace to embrace God's reconciled reality in order to experience God's will for our lives.

A further explanation concerning the inheritance of salvation (4:1-7). Paul offered by analogy another argument concerning the irrelevance of the Law for those who have received the Spirit of God's Son. The analogy builds off the matter of minors who become heirs before they reach the age of their majority. Paul reasoned that an heir is always an heir, but as a minor an heir is not yet vested in the inheritance; instead, guardians or trustees are set over the heir *until* the appointed time of inheritance. Paul's application of this image to the matter of Christian life is almost an allegory. He identified the "heirs" as those of Faith who were like minors before God sent Christ. In turn, the "guardians" of humanity prior to the advent of Christ were "elemental spirits of the universe": Paul did not specify the identity of these spirits, but in reflecting on his subsequent statements one can see that (a) for Gentiles, Paul meant to name lesser gods, demons, etc.; and (b) for Jews, he meant the Law. Above all, Paul's focus on the Law as an elemental spirit of the universe was meant to dissociate the Law from God. The Law served a purpose, but the Law is not to be directly associated with God any more than are lesser gods and demons.

Paul continued by focusing on the matter of the appointed time of inheritance. He identified that time with God's sending of Christ. Thus, Paul reasoned that those of faith are now fully vested and, therefore, free and without need for the Law. The way Paul crafted his argument is powerful. The idea of God's sending his Son, Christ, for the purpose of saving humanity occur here and in Rom 8:3-4. Paul was actually taking up a motif from Hellenistic Judaism, that of God's sending a savior for humanity's sake. Outside the Old Testament in the Jewish writings of the Hellenistic period one sees in Philo, *Dreams* 1.69; Sirach 24; Baruch 3; and Wisdom 9 the idea that *God acted by sending a savior in order to bring salvation*, although in these places God sent "Wisdom" or the "Logos" as the agent of salvation. Paul picked up this abstract, mythical theme and made it concrete: "God acted for the salvation of humanity by sending a savior" = *God sent God's Son, Jesus Christ, to redeem humanity so we might receive adoption as children of God*. The once hopeful thought is declared to be a reality; the mythical figure Wisdom is simply replaced by the humanly born, real Son of God, Jesus Christ. Paul transformed a pattern of wishful thinking into a metaphor for declaring the reality of the gospel of God's salvation in Jesus Christ brought into being in the context of real human existence.

[One comment here as an aside: Recent, contemporary infatuation with the figure of Wisdom, primarily because the word for "wisdom" in Greek is the feminine form *sophia*, is nothing more than an attempt to regress behind the reality of the gospel to the mythic themes of ancient religious speculation–"Wisdom" is no more relevant for Christians today than the Law was for the first-century Galatians. What matters for Christians is the reality of Christ.]

Further argument (4:8-11). Paul's discussion in these verses extends from the last analogy. Prior to their conversion the Galatians were pagans who would most likely have worshiped idols. Paul informed them that, as Christians, they were freed *from* idols as they were freed *in Christ*. Paul identified the desire of the Galatians to become Law-observant as nothing but a desire to return to bondage. In fact, the Galatians probably only wanted some clear instructions about how to regulate their relationship to God, that is, some directions about how they should live their lives. They saw no danger in this desire, but Paul did!

Verses 8-9 are crucial. Paul started to speak in a "normal" way by reflecting on the reality of salvation *from a human angle*; but, abruptly, he stopped in mid-sentence and corrected the error of his own logic by speaking *of the divine angle* on salvation. The divine has priority over the human in the reality of salvation, although the human angle exists and is important. We should remember in reflecting on these lines today that whether or not we think idols are lesser gods or demons, the Galatians probably did—and Paul used their assumptions, which he may have shared, to create distress that aims at bringing the Galatians back to where Paul wanted them to be, namely, in a vital relationship to God with full confidence in God's involvement with and direction of their lives. The Galatians needed, and we today need, to trust God and not to turn to religious regulations.

Paul's further appeal to the Galatians (4:12-20). With rhetoric, Paul transported the Galatians back to a holy moment in their past, to the origin of their faith. He reminded them of their reception of the gospel, and he reminded them of their gracious reception of the apostle himself (despite his troublesome condition at the time). Then, Paul made an emotional appeal. Notice, Paul's plea was not based on guilt; rather, he appealed to their hearts as he continued to appeal to their heads. The metaphors here are thick, but Paul's point is clear: He wanted the Galatians to remember and reaffirm the gospel (the good news of God's having sent Christ for the salvation of humanity) as they had first heard and believed it, that is, without regard for the Law and in Faith brought by the presence and the power of the Spirit. Paul wanted the Galatians to trust God fully, not to try to supplement God's work of salvation with their own efforts.

It is easy to misunderstand Paul at this juncture. His disregard for Law-observance could be taken to mean that he did not think that how humans live makes any difference in the divine scheme of things. Nothing could be further from the truth. For Paul, God's salvation has a profound impact on human life. Christian life is not a religious joyride. God cares about humanity; and so we are called to obedience, to faithfulness, to the living of transformed lives. But such living is the experience, not the achievement or the maintenance, of God's salvation. Thus, we must continue to follow Paul as he wrote to the Galatians about the preservation of the truth of the gospel.

A full-fledged allegory (4:21-31). Paul declared that his argument in these verses was an allegory (Gal 4:24). Again, he took up material from the story of Abraham, but then Paul considered the larger family story by focusing on the two sons and the two "wives" of Abraham. First, there is Isaac, who was born by Sarah —who is not named here, but who is called the free woman. Isaac was born by or through God's promise, and his birth was something of a miracle, for in Gal 4:29 Paul said that Isaac was born "according to the Spirit." Second, there is Ishmael—who is not named here—who was born of Hagar, who is called "the slave." Ishmael was born "according to the Flesh," that is, outside the promise of God and the miraculous work of the Spirit.

Once again, Paul created sets of opposites: Flesh/Spirit; slave/free; Flesh/promise. Paul allegorized both the story of Abraham's family and the sets of opposites as he interpreted and applied the account to the situation in Galatia. As Paul worked out his allegory we see that Hagar, the slave, represents Mount Sinai where the Law was given; and she represents the Jerusalem of the present where "false believers" (the preachers in Galatia?) tried to spy on freedom in Christ Jesus. Paul declared that the children of

Hagar (Sinai = Law; Jerusalem = Law-observance) are children of slavery. By contrast, the free woman Sarah represents the Jerusalem above (God's realm and the place from which divine intervention for salvation comes) who bears children of the promised blessing (those who, like Abraham, believe and are blessed by believing).

Moreover, Paul tapped the rich vein of Jewish legend as he continued his argument. One should recall that in Genesis Sarah merely saw the slave son and insisted that he and his mother be sent away. According to Jewish legend, however, Ishmael persecuted Isaac. Paul said it was the same way in Galatia: The Law-observant opposed and oppressed those who were Law-free in Christ. Finally, Paul gave an overt proof-text for his advice: "Cast out the slave and her son"; that is, Paul said to be done with Law-observance, for it has no inheritance in the age of the promise which is the age of the Spirit. With the Spirit really present, the Christian has no need for the Law.

Paul's theme (5:1). Paul moved forcefully from allegory to state his point directly: Christians are freed by Christ for freedom —an exhilarating, liberating, frightening condition. The substance of Christian freedom is not stated here, but in the following elaborate statements about the Spirit one gets a clear idea of what freedom is. We should see in relation to this crucial verse (Gal 5:1) that Christians are freed by Christ; but the freedom requires some effort—Christians must resist all forms of spiritual slavery that reduce their association with God to anything other than a vital, direct, living, Spirit-direct relationship. Paul issued this warning against taking on a yoke of slavery because it is easy to be enslaved by forms of spirituality that present prescriptions and proscriptions rather than issue a call to the paradox of freedom and obligation.

A warning (5:2-4). Paul said that moving toward Law-observance denies Christ and the freedom he grants. In addition, Paul informed the Galatians that there is no such thing as a little human-ly-maintained systemic righteousness. Paul sharply juxtaposed justification "by Law" that is a humanly maintained religious status with justification "by grace" that is created, granted, and sustained by God.

The correct Christian posture for life (5:5-6). Paul declared that by the power of the Spirit and out of faith, Christians await the hope of righteousness—which is God's. Faith is the source of hope as God is the source of salvation. Verse 6 summarizes Paul's thematic concern, "For in Christ neither circumcision not uncircumcision matters anything, but faith is working through love." Thus, human religious status does not mean salvation; rather, humans experience the quality of life that God intends as Faith energizes a new way of living that is made real through love.

More comments on the Galatian situation (5:7-12). The Galatians were doing fine, but under the influence of those advocating Law-observance they were now "hindered." Their own interest in Law-observance did not originate with God. Yet, in Gal 5:10 Paul expressed his confidence; and then, suddenly he became obviously impassioned in 5:11, declaring that Law-observance removes the scandal of the cross—denying the sufficiency of what God had done through the saving death of Jesus Christ. Thus, in 5:12 Paul uttered a crude wish for his adversaries in Galatia: The NRSV translates, "I wish those who unsettle you would castrate themselves." Apparently Paul meant sarcastically to say that if a little circumcision is a good thing, why not go all the way!

Galatians 5:13–6:18

Paul obviously had confidence that the Galatians would come around to his understanding, for the letter moves in the last major segments into a didactic style. The major efforts at persuasion were done, and now Paul settled down to teach the Galatian churches.

The use of freedom (5:13-15). Called to freedom, the Galatians were told they could use their freedom as an opportunity either to focus on themselves or to focus on others. Paul implied that the true test of religion is its focus on the self or on others. In Gal 5:14 Paul repeated a well-known line from Lev 19:18. Paul's fondness for this portion of the Old Testament is clear, for the line from Leviticus also lies behind his remarks in Rom 13:8-10. The popularity and importance of this line in early Christianity may stem from the use of Leviticus by Jesus himself, who is found uttering this line in Matt 22:39 and Mark 12:31; compare Luke 10:27. Here, Paul taught that genuine religion directs one toward others rather than merely toward one's self.

Galatians 5:15 offers a practical word for living, but it is a strange, enigmatic remark in this context—perhaps anticipating what the apostle would say in Gal 6:1-5. Paul seems to have warned against bickering in the life of the church, or perhaps, against a kind of spiritual comparison that pits one believer against another in a competitive manner that produces destructive hostility.

Spirit and Flesh (5:16-24). Paul reasoned like a rabbi as he pondered the Spirit and the Flesh in relation, or better, in opposition to each other. The rabbis taught that humans were under the influence of two distinct "impulses" (called *yetzers*). One impulse was good, the other evil. Humans had to resist the evil impulse as they yielded to the urgings of the good. Paul did not write of *yetzers*, but he presented Spirit and Flesh in an antithetical relationship as powers that influence human behavior. Paul plainly called for the Galatians to *walk in the Spirit*, a genuinely charismatic form of life that means following the leadership of the Spirit, so that believers will have no need for a Law that would simply tell them what to do and not to do. Furthermore, Paul said those in the realm of the Spirit's influence are *not* under the Law.

Paul made two lists, "the works of the Flesh" and "the fruit of the Spirit." Such catalogues were the stock materials of the moral teachings of Hellenistic philosophers, so that Paul's rabbinic meditation on "impulses" gives way to plainer, more prosaic teaching. The works of the Flesh are listed in 5:19-21, and Paul gave a blunt warning, "The ones practicing these things shall not inherit the kingdom of God." In turn, in 5:22-23 Paul listed the fruit of the Spirit. One should note that Paul wrote "fruit," not "fruits." His singular form indicates that he understood the characteristics and qualities listed here to be traits that are to be manifested in the lives of *all* believers. Thus, the fruit of the Spirit is not to be equated with Paul's lists of "gifts of the Spirit" that are found in other letters.

In this list of the fruit of the Spirit, one should notice that in 5:22 Paul listed *pistis*, that is, "faith." Translations usually render *pistis* as "faithfulness," but Paul knew a word for faithfulness that he used elsewhere, but not here. In the context of Galatians Paul was making the important point that Faith itself comes into the lives of believers through the presence and the power of the Spirit —as do all the qualities listed as "fruit of the Spirit."

Finally, Gal 5:24 is an observation: Christians are freed from the Flesh. For the sake of understanding, to put it another way for clarity, Paul said that all in all you can judge a tree by the fruit it bears.

An admonition about the Spirit (5:25-26). Gal 5:25 literally says, in a conditional sentence that states terms, "If we live in (or 'by') the Spirit, indeed in (or 'by') the Spirit let us stay in line." Paul's language is metaphorical, employing technical terminology for the formation of a line by a military unit. Plainly he said that Christian freedom is not joyful anarchy; rather, the Spirit frees us and forms us according to the parameters of God's will. In turn, Gal 5:26 is an exhortation in negative form that builds off the previous statement. Put positively, Paul asserted that Christians are to live *humbly, sensitively,* and *appreciatively* in relation to one another.

Christian living (6:1-5). Paul's directions become remarkably practical as he reasoned about the life of the members of the Galatian congregations. Paul taught that in dealing with those in the wrong, Christians are to "be gentle." Why? From a purely practical perspective, the answer is that *all go wrong.* From a theological perspective, however, Christians correct one another in gentleness because *Christ himself bore our burdens*; so now—as he did, so are we to—bear one another's burdens. Furthermore, Paul argued that to commit one's life to Christ is to be done with self-deception, for now we live our lives—not for ourselves, but—for Christ, our Lord. Christians are called to responsibility, not to minding one another's business in an effort to judge ourselves better than others. We stand in a direct relationship to God, and for us life is not merely a matter of how we appear in comparison with everyone else.

Generosity and support (6:6). This line may be a specific teaching, but in the context of the discussion in Galatians Paul seems to have offered a general and deliberately ambiguous admonition to live life giving support to the ministry of teaching. One should recall here that Paul made it his practice in relation to the congregations among which he labored not to accept pay. Clearly, then, he was not soliciting a contribution; although he may have recognized the fact that the mission of the church in the world is done at a real cost.

More observations and advice (6:7-10). Paul continued with several related points. In general, we should remember that through these four verses Paul's concern was with inner-church relations. First, Christians cannot con God. Second, when we focus on ourselves, even in God's name, we have the wrong priorities and we stand condemned (by God). Third, vigorous involvement with the Spirit is the right way for believers to go about life—and such living, charismatic as it is, produces the practical results in our lives that God desires. Fourth, Paul recognized the reality that it is often hard to do what is right; and he encouraged and reminded the Galatians that faithful devotion to God's will insures the final, right results.

Paul's final words (6:11-18). Paul brought the letter to a conclusion with his own hand rather than by continuing to use the services of the secretary (or amanuensis) who had obviously been taking Paul's dictation up to this point. His mention of the large letters with which he wrote may mean nothing more than that he did not have the fine, trained hand of a professional scribe. Nevertheless, this so-called autograph gave a genuinely personal touch to the letter.

As he wrote, Paul once again confronted the tendency toward Law-observance that he battled through the earlier sections of the letter. He put a new twist on the point that he made at Gal 5:11, observing that concern with Law-observance is a style of living that actively avoids the danger and the scandal of the cross of Christ. Paul seems to have suggested that it is easy to feel religious while doing little that matters, in fact, it is a way to avoid Christian responsibility by being seemingly, though irrelevantly, devout. Paul was candid as he suggested that the Law-observant preachers who advocated circumcision were wrong and that they were seeking the security of persuading others to join them in their erroneous concerns.

Paul exposed the false glory of Law-observance by pointing to the real glory of selfless, self-sacrificial love that is the true characteristic of God's own love and the evidence of the presence of the Spirit within believers. Paul said the practice of circumcision is truly vain in comparison with the new order or creation that has come as a divinely instituted reality through the cross of the Lord Jesus Christ. From his perspective in the time of the new creation, Paul declared that those unconcerned with circumcision who live out of the reality of the cross of Christ are those who do God's will as "the Israel of God."

In a penultimate remark (Gal 6:17), Paul disavowed those who opposed him, and as he declared his freedom from concern with such persons he referred to the physical signs of his suffering in obedience to Christ. Finally, Paul ended the letter as he had begun it, that is, with a thoroughly theological statement, a benediction. Viewing the Galatians as a united living entity, Paul called for "the grace of our Lord Jesus Christ" (see Gal 1:3) to be with the "spirit" of the Galatians. Christ's grace brought the Galatian congregations into existence, and the presence and power of the Spirit united them and sustained them in faith.

Recommended for Further Study

The study of Galatians presents several challenges for the preacher and teacher. One major challenge has to do with theology, and another with history.

The theological challenge roots in the Protestant tradition itself, which to a large extent has been shaped by the Reformers' (especially Luther's) reading of Paul's letters to the Galatians and to the Romans. The problem lies in hearing Paul's voice over that of the Reformers who have interpreted him. Moving beyond their assumption that the doctrine of justification by faith not only underlies Galatians but the whole of Paul's theology is not easy, but move we must in order to hear the full message of the apostle, especially his apocalyptically shaped urgency and confidence. Marion Soards' introduction in the previous chapter is a good place to begin; the sources listed in the section below, "Understanding Paul," are good places to continue the quest.

The historical challenge roots also in the Protestant tradition in the tendency to view Paul's experience with Jewish Christianity through the lens of Luther's sixteenth-century clash with the Roman Catholic Church. During the past fifteen years, in particular, we have learned to see the Jews and Jewish Christians of the first century in new light. Our understanding of the varieties of Jewish systems of belief and practice has grown, as has our sense of the role of the Law within those systems. Again, Soards indicates this change of perspective in his introduction, and more can be learned about the state of scholarship on the issue by considering the works listed in "Paul and the Law."

Also listed below are commentaries and other resources helpful for the preaching and teaching tasks.

Understanding Paul

Beker, J. Christian. *Paul the Apostle: The Triumph of God in Life and Thought*. Philadelphia: Fortress Press, 1980.

Bornkamm, Günther. *Paul*. Translated by D. M. G. Stalker. New York: Harper and Row, 1971.

Schoeps, Hans Joachim. *Paul. The Theology of the Apostle in the Light of Jewish Religious History*. Translated by Harold Knight. Philadelphia: Westminster Press, 1961.

Soards, Marion L. *The Apostle Paul: An Introduction to His Writings and Teaching*. New York: Paulist Press, 1987.

Stendahl, Krister. *Paul among Jews and Gentiles and Other Essays*. Philadelphia: Fortress Press, 1976.

Schweitzer, Albert. *The Mysticism of Paul the Apostle*. Translated by William Montgomery. New York: Henry Holt & Co., 1931.

Paul and the Law

Davies, W. D. *Paul and Rabbinic Judaism: Some Rabbinic Elements in Pauline Theology*. 4th ed. Philadelphia: Fortress Press, 1980.

Drane, John W. *Paul: Libertine or Legalist? A Study in the Theology of the Major Pauline Epistles*. London: SPCK, 1975.

Dunn, James D. G. *Jesus, Paul, and the Law. Studies in Mark and Galatians*. Louisville: Westminster/John Knox, 1990.

Luedemann, Gerd. *Opposition to Paul in Jewish Christianity.* Translated by M. Eugene Boring. Minneapolis: Fortress Press, 1989.

Räisänen, Heikki. *Paul and the Law.* Philadelphia: Fortress Press, 1983.

Sanders, E. P. *Paul, the Law, and the Jewish People.* Philadelphia: Fortress Press, 1983.

Thematic Studies

Bassler, Jouette M., editor. *Pauline Theology. Volume One: Thessalonians, Philippians, Galatians, Philemon.* Minneapolis: Augsburg Fortress, 1991.

Cosgrove, Charles H. *The Cross and the Spirit: A Study in the Argument and Theology of Galatians.* Macon GA: Mercer University Press, 1988.

Furnish, Victor Paul. *Theology and Ethics in Paul.* Nashville: Abingdon Press, 1968.

Hays, Richard B. "Christology and Ethics in Galatians: The Law of Christ." *The Catholic Biblical Quarterly* 49:2 (1987): 268-90.

Howard, George. *Paul: Crisis in Galatia. A Study in Early Christian Theology.* Society for New Testament Studies Monograph Series 35. Cambridge: Cambridge University Press, 1978.

Lategan, Bernard C. "Is Paul Developing a Specifically Christian Ethics in Galatians?" in *Greeks, Romans, and Christians:*

Essays in Honor of Abraham J. Malherbe. Edited by David L. Balch, et al. Minneapolis: Augsburg Fortress, 1990.

Neyrey, Jerome H., S.J. "Bewitched in Galatia: Paul and Cultural Anthropology." *The Catholic Biblical Quarterly* 50:1 (1988): 72-100.

Olson, Mark J. *Galatians: In Defense of Love*. Macon GA: Smyth & Helwys Publishing, Inc., 1994.

Walker, William O. "Why Paul Went to Jerusalem: The Interpretation of Galatians 2:1-5." *The Catholic Biblical Quarterly* 54:3 (1992): 503-10.

Williams, Sam K. "*Promise* in Galatians: A Reading of Paul's Reading of Scripture." *Journal of Biblical Literature* 107:4 (1988): 709-20.

Commentaries

Betz, Hans Dieter. *Galatians: A Commentary on Paul's Letter to the Churches in Galatia*. Hermeneia. Philadelphia: Fortress Press, 1979.

Bruce, F. F. *The Epistle to the Galatians*. Grand Rapids: Wm. B. Eerdmans, 1963.

Burton, Ernest De Witt. *A Critical and Exegetical Commentary on the Epistle to the Galatians*. International Critical Commentary. Edinburgh: T. & T. Clark, 1921.

Cosgrove, Charles H. "Galatians." *Mercer Commentary on the Bible*. Macon GA: Mercer University Press, 1994.

Duncan, George S. *The Epistle of Paul to the Galatians*. Moffatt New Testament Commentary. London: Hodder and Stoughton, 1934.

Guthrie, Donald. *Galatians*. New Century Bible. London: Marshall, Morgan, & Scott, 1981.

Lightfoot, J. B. *St. Paul's Epistle to the Galatians*. Lynn MA: Hendrickson Publishers, Inc., 1981.

Lührmann, Dieter. *Galatians*. A Continental Commentary. Translated by O. C. Dean, Jr. Minneapolis: Fortress Press, 1992.

Homiletical and Devotional Resources

Cousar, Charles B. *Galatians*. Interpretation: A Bible Commentary for Teaching and Preaching. Atlanta: John Knox, 1982.

Harrisville, Roy A. "Galatians 5:1." *Interpretation: A Journal of Bible and Theology* 37:3 (1983): 288-93.

Hubbard, David Alan. *Galatians: Gospel of Freedom*. Waco: Word Books, 1977.

Patte, Daniel. *Preaching Paul*. Fortress Resources for Preaching. Philadelphia: Fortress, 1984.

Stagg, Frank. *Galatians. Romans*. Knox Preaching Guides. Atlanta: John Knox Press, 1980.

Trentham, Charles A. "Preaching from Galatians." *Review & Expositor* 69:4 (1972): 495-506.

There Is
No Other Gospel

Galatians 1:1-10

Mark E. Hopper

Paul wasted no time with the Galatian Christians. He quickly got to the heart of his great concern about them. After the obligatory opening greeting of his letter, forsaking the likewise customary thanksgiving portion of fond remembrances, the apostle vented his anger in brittle fashion: "I am amazed that you are so quickly deserting him who called you in the grace of Christ and turning to a different gospel." But there is more. The gospel Paul defended was intimately tied to his person, to his own call as an apostle, a proclaimer of this very gospel under attack. The gospel, the gospel's apostle, and the gospel's Lord all came in package form. To buy one was to buy all. And at least in this case, to attack one was to attack all.

Why all the fuss? Because in Paul's words, "there is no other gospel." Not in all the known world does another gospel exist. Not then, not now. The good news that Paul preached to the Galatians was one that declared the great liberty and freedom from sin, which is found in Christ alone. There is no other gospel.

Of course this gospel *has* been changed, turned into perversions many times throughout history. In the Galatian experience, however, some unknown persons were evidently preaching that in order to perfect the Christian experience, circumcision was necessary. Their message was Christ plus circumcision guarantees salvation and the ability to live morally pure lives. If the Galatian Christians were struggling with the demands of living out their calling in a hostile world, this gospel-turned-into-its-opposite would have been appealing and would have gained a foothold in the community of faith.

The very center of the issue was and is the nature of the gospel: is it legalism or grace? Paul's opponents argued for the necessity of law-keeping in addition to personal commitment to Christ; Paul insisted upon the sufficiency of Christ "who gave himself for our sins to set us free from the present evil age." This thought alone states Paul's case:

> There is no other gospel. In Jesus God gave himself on our behalf for the purpose of gaining our freedom from the power of sin not only in the future, but in the here and now. To add anything to this gospel is anathema to the apostle. There just isn't any other gospel.

I must admit that while I have never preached "Christ plus circumcision," I nevertheless at times have come close to substituting some other kind of gospel in place of the one "who gave himself for our sins in order to deliver us from the present evil age." After all, I am an American. It is most difficult for me to believe in grace, in unconditional love and acceptance before God. Too many times, I fall victim to the gospels of self-sufficiency, of capitalism, of you-earn-what-you-get, of achievement, of success-is-growth syndromes. These are all perversions of the good news about Jesus Christ. Shallow American Christianity has been uncritical in its thinking about the substance of the gospel. All too frequently we substitute style for substance, delivery for content, denominational correct thinking for message. Such are the brands of our own legalism, of law-keeping. We, too, deny the gospel even as we cling to our non-gospels. If the Galatians misunderstood the heart of the Christian faith, we have done the same. Like them, we have it backwards. It is not what *we* can do to overcome our moral failures; it is what God has done for us in Christ that "delivers us from this present evil age." There is no other gospel than the gospel of grace.

The words of the text must come alive in the experience of the church again! It is impossible for any other gospel to save us. And yet the very simplicity of the message is notoriously difficult to preach or believe. Grace. Unconditional love. The freedom of acceptance. How difficult!

I minister in a capital city. It is a very political city. The local politics of place are magnified in that it is a small city. Government is not immersed in other pursuits of livelihood. Government and political life make the city. At election time it is a well-established practice for political candidates to make the rounds of the local church communities in order to be seen, to make contacts, to campaign. The practice has always bothered me.

In one frank conversation I had with an elected official (not from my city), I was surprised at her candor. She spoke of attending a worship service in one of the mega-churches in our state, looking around at the thousands of gathered worshipers, and saying to herself, "If you were running for office from this district, you'd be crazy not to go to church here. Just look at all the votes!" To her credit she hastened to add that such thinking would not be proper motivation to join a church. But you see the temptation. The use of the gospel for personal gain will always be a perversion of the death of Christ on our behalf to free us from this present evil age.

Paul said as much in the last verse of our text: "Am I now seeking human approval, or God's approval? Or am I trying to please people? If I were still pleasing people, I would not be a servant of Christ." Paul saved his self-designation as slave of Christ until the very end of this opening section. Normally it came in his opening sentence. It is quite clear that if one is truly a "slave of Christ," the gospel can never be used for personal gain of any sort. The point is made by Charles Cousar:

> All positions of leadership are in danger of becoming power bases where people satisfy their own needs, manipulate and even oppress others, and make certain that decisions turn out "our" way (never mind about God's way). In ecclesiastical circles the gospel may even be

cleverly or unconsciously used to keep recalcitrants in line. Thus the simple question about service and accountability to God is always an appropriate question to ask oneself. Faced honestly, it will painfully expose human pretense, but at the same time will point toward true freedom.[1]

In a political context (or in any other context of life), here is the power of the one true gospel to shatter human pretense, transform human, and make it new in the image of Christ, enabling the believer to find Christian freedom in a hostile world. Augmentation to this gospel is neither necessary nor possible. In only the way Martin Luther could do it, his statement still holds true: "That which does not teach Christ is not apostolic, even if Peter and Paul be the teachers. On the other hand, that which does teach Christ is apostolic, even if Judas, Annas, Pilate, or Herod should propound it."

The call to proclaim Christ and Christ alone is the only credential one needs to be qualified as preacher. In a world of professionalism, expertise, qualification, the "outsider" with no credentialing from the approved official sources (other than a certain message from God) troubles us. In the early church's experience of roving bands of prophets, charismatic leaders, and itinerant preachers, they struggled with the issues of messenger and message. Things were messy. Church life and doctrine slowly took shape. Organizational flow charts began to develop, but they were not all the same. The Spirit moved as it willed. However imperfect, the church in its entirety is the repository of the apostolic message and the historical struggle to define the message and validate the messenger. The result is this: it is not the messenger that validates the message, it is always the message that validates the messenger. This is eternally so because the church's proclamation, in apostolic form, tells of the One "who gave himself for our sins in order to deliver us from the present evil age."

Perhaps we have become so enamored with degrees and authentication from proper channels that credential the messenger, we now find ourselves in the position of honoring the messenger over the message, of experiencing church as a personality cult. "Gospel experts" have taken control over church life, biblical interpretation, and application to life. Again, the freedom of the gospel alone to qualify and authenticate the messenger has been lost to us in exchange for a different type of legalism: "professionalism."

God calls whom God wills, apart from human agency. Ms. Emma is a woman in her early eighties. She still works part-time in a cafeteria in a government office building. Not only is she still active in the labor force, she is also still active in extraordinary Christian service. She bakes cookies for any church group (from youth to senior adults) going on a church mission. She works in our church's clothes closet. She actively visits the sick in hospitals and nursing homes. She personally helps deliver needed clothes, food, and toys to a mission in the mountains of Kentucky. She hosts a mission study society in her home. Every Sunday morning, she leads a worship service in a nursing home, enlisting others to play the piano, bring the patients, share the gospel.

Can you picture her? When *she* rises in our congregation to speak about missions, people stop and listen as in the old E. F. Hutton commercial. Why? Because she bears the only qualification necessary to speak. To be sure, she is a saint. But more importantly, she is God-called to speak and bear witness to the One who delivers us from our present evil age. She carries about her the essence of the gospel, for she herself is gift, is grace to us. Sometimes she troubles us with her words of challenge. But she, too, is a servant of Christ, and her message is apostolic. Thus it is that she always empowers us toward freedom and a responsible discipleship. For her, as for Paul, there is only one gospel.

The God who raised Christ from the dead is the same God who gives to us the gifts of grace and peace through faith in Christ. Grace. Peace. Could there possibly be anything more needed in our world today? How tragically sad we have become in our various attempts to supplement God's free gift of himself and dictate for ourselves or others some particular accomplishment that becomes a "must."

Still, there is always hope for us. Possibilities remain that we can shed our legalisms and secular cynicism for the gospel of God's graciousness. God is for us! Christ died for our sins! We are delivered from the power of this evil age! In the very midst of conflict and turmoil, the apostle Paul, through these affirmations, reminded the Galatian Christians and us that only one thing matters in life—the word about the death and resurrection of Christ is *all* we need in order to find our way to grace, to peace, the very things we lack and most need. When it comes to choosing legalism of any kind over God's grace in Christ, Paul made the only choice possible. He chose grace. For after all, there is no other gospel.

Note

[1]*Galatians*, Interpretation: A Commentary for Teaching and Preaching (Atlanta: John Knox, 1982) 24.

The Courage to Stand for Liberty

Galatians 1:11–2:14

Thomas R. McKibbens

The story given in Galatians 1:11–2:14, in case anyone failed to see the fireworks, was a first-hand account of a near knock-down, drag-out church fight between two leading Christian leaders. That's always news—both then and now. Somewhere down deep we must still hold the notion that Christian community means Christian agreement, and that church meetings should always consist of smiles and sweetness and glad hands. Then when the reality hits us in the face, we are surprised. Maybe deep down we think that we can't be both Christian and human.

I.

The fight began innocently enough—with a life story. And since it was Paul telling the story, he confined it to his own, not his opponent's. It is a story that covers roughly two decades of his life, and the upshot of the story is that Paul preached to the Gentiles on the authority of God, not the authority of the Jerusalem church leaders. ". . . I did not confer with any human being, nor did I go up to Jerusalem to those who were already apostles before me, but I went away at once into Arabia, and afterwards I returned to Damascus," he said (Gal 1:16-17). He was already getting a little testy.

Finally, he said that he met in Jerusalem with Peter for fifteen days, and apparently Peter (at least by implication) had no problem with Paul's work. So off Paul went to continue his preaching mission. Fourteen years went by, and who knows what news reached the Jerusalem leaders about Paul's work. That he was successful in starting churches was beyond dispute. That he encouraged an egalitarian style of ministry with regard to race and social class and gender was without doubt. It is no accident that this letter holds high the egalitarian banner: "There is no longer Jew or Greek, there is no longer slave or free, there is no longer male or female: for all of you are one in Christ Jesus" (3:28).

And after fourteen years of this liberal preaching, that egalitarianism could very well have been behind the Jerusalem rumblings about his ministry that likely prompted his return to the city. So he described his return visit to Jerusalem, and this time he took off the gloves. He told it like it was (and frequently still is).

He told of a meeting with the Jerusalem church leaders, and between the lines we can see all kinds of things going on. "I laid before them the gospel that I proclaim among the Gentiles," he said (2:2). He was obviously talking about his egalitarian preaching, which could not be easily swallowed by the Jerusalem conservatives. But his liberalism seemed not to phase the leaders. To Paul's surprise, they did not even try to have Paul's Gentile companion, Titus, circumcized according to the Jewish law. Apparently, the leaders were satisfied that Paul's preaching was genuinely Christian. They may have even been a little jealous that Paul could preach such egalitarianism with no reprisals from the church members.

But there was deception in the ranks. The super-conservatives in the church were not satisfied with the word of their leaders. They had to make sure that Paul's orthodoxy suited theirs. So they placed spies in the meeting, people whom Paul called "false believers secretely brought in, who slipped in to spy on the freedom we have in Christ Jesus, so that they might enslave us" (2:4). It's the same old story: super-conservatives who don't trust their representatives to make informed decisions. But Paul did not waver in the face of opposition from anyone: ". . . we did not submit to them even for a moment," he claimed. He refused to sit on the fence, to find a happy medium, to pacify the conservatives, to use what Ralph Elliott has called "doublespeak." So off he went back to Antioch to preach as he had been preaching for all those years.

II.

That was Paul's story. But now what about his opponent in the church fight—Peter, whose life story is not told in this account? What about him? He, of all the apostles, comes across as the most human. He liked to fish, but he was more attracted to Jesus than to his father's fishing fleet. He became such good friends with Jesus that he earned a nickname—Rock—and tradition says that the church would be built on people with faith like Peter's.

What kind of faith was that? To be blunt, it was a very human faith. It was a faith that would think nothing of jumping out of a boat to walk with Jesus on water, but a faith human enough to yell out in fear when he started sinking down (Matt 14:28-31). It was a faith loving enough to claim that though everybody else might desert Jesus, he would never fall away, and then turn right around on the same night and deny Jesus three times (Matt 26).

It was a faith, in other words, that was willing to believe the impossible. And that was precisely what he was called upon to believe. His orthodox Jewish faith thought it was impossible for a Gentile to be a part of the community of faith. Yet on a trip to Caesarea he discovered the impossible. A Roman soldier named Cornelius was converted and baptized. And Peter for the first time realized the truth that the gospel was not just for Jews, but also for Gentiles. He did the unthinkable: he actually sat down and ate with Gentiles. No longer did he see them as Gentiles, but as part of his family of faith. It was as though a great wall was removed. Here—at last—was Jew and Gentile standing side by side as equals (Acts 10).

This scene is perhaps the most crucial moment in the life of the early church. Peter's courage allowed the gospel to break out of its Jewish corral and gallop with head held high over every hilltop of the world. That is the kind of faith and inspired openness on which the church is built.

III.

So it must have been a great day when both Paul and Peter—two men with such courageous biographies—came to meet in Antioch. It must have warmed Peter's heart to leave the confines of the Jerusalem church and travel to Antioch where he could see people of different races and different social classes and different genders sit down as equals—brothers and sisters in the church. What a liberating experience! What a transforming experience!

But Peter had a problem. As liberating as that must have been for him in Antioch, there was a "separate but equal" group back in Jerusalem. They were very vocal, very sincere Jewish Christians. But they were apparently more Jewish than Christian. Their argument went like this:

> Let the Gentiles have their church and we'll have ours. They probably wouldn't like the way we worship anyway. Let's be nice to them, but whatever you do, don't invite them home to dinner! That breaks our most sacred traditions.

As though this group did not trust Peter away from home, they sent a delegation (translate it as "spies") to Antioch presumably to check out the orthodoxy of the church, but likely also to check out Peter's orthodoxy. Any how, when they arrived in Antioch, Peter conveniently disappeared at dinner time! After all, Peter had to live with these people! Here is the sarcastic way Paul described the scene: "But after they came, [Peter] drew back and kept himself separate for fear of the circumcision faction" (2:12). The cowardice of Peter in the face of criticism began to rebuild the very wall that Peter himself had helped destroy earlier.

This is the point at which Paul stepped in and "opposed him to his face" (2:11). He had to! The whole future of the church was in danger. Paul challenged him: "How can you be such a hypocrite?" We don't know Peter's answer. Surely he was humiliated; surely he knew deep down that he was wrong. The church in Antioch—the church of liberty—eventually eclipsed the Jerusalem church and became the home base for all of Paul's journeys. From that church grew some of the greatest thinkers of the early centuries.

IV.

From our vantage point it is very easy to condemn Peter for his hypocracy. Who can fail to see it? How could a person be more human than to bow to the pressure of criticism? What is more human than to reverse our position when it becomes unpopular? We can hardly help but be sympathetic to Peter. He was in an extremely difficult position. No one is questioning his genuine Christian faith or his commitment. He wanted peace in the church. We all do, and who among us has failed to compromise to achieve peace?

But the question posed so sharply in this story is where we draw the line in such compromise? How far do we bend in order to maintain peace between conservatives and liberals, between law and freedom? The history of the church is largely the story of that struggle. There is no doubt on which side the letter of Galatians stands in this struggle. The freedom on Antioch stands head and shoulders over the legalism of Jerusalem. That is beyound question in Galatians.

What is at issue is our own courage, or failure of courage, when we face the same struggle today. The vision of race, class, and gender equality in the church is far from achieved, and the struggle to achieve it becomes even more acute when the opponents come not from without, but from within. How far we bend is something we each have to determine for ourselves.

V.

But this I know: the letter of Galatians is no comfort for the self-appointed guardians of orthodoxy in any church. It is no comfort for the proponents of church growth based on one class and race. It is no comfort for those supporting male dominance in the church. Galatians lifts high the banner of liberty and equality in the church, a banner under which we can stand only with greatest faith and courage.

The Grace of Faithfulness

Galatians 2:11-21

Howard W. Roberts

Whenever two or three people get together, at least five or six opinions will be expressed. Of course, the quotation most associated with two or three people gathering together is the promise of God to be in the middle of the gathering. God being present does not preclude there being five or six opinions. Actually, it is more the norm that if people gather in God's name to be God's people, there will be a variety of opinions because people are uniquely made by God. People relating to and worshiping God leads to unity but not uniformity.

Have there been times in your life when you thought surely the church is a place where no arguments, disagreements, or conflicts occur? What was the basis for this kind of thinking? Perhaps it was the desire to find a place of quiet rest. Maybe you were at a point in your life when you needed a safe place to be where people would not be out to destroy each other. The church can be and needs to be this kind of place, but that does not preclude differences of opinion and conflict. What the church needs to do is always be on the lookout for creative ways to resolve conflict. We in the church need to find ways to receive grace and to give grace. This is what the text in Galatians 2:11-21 expresses.

We are indebted to members of the early church for their willingness to expose their diversty of opinion and allow us to see some of the conflicts with which they struggled. The awareness of conflict and arguments among people like Peter, James, Paul, and Barnabas usually shocks the novice and the naive. But boldly and clearly Paul wrote that he and Peter had a major disagreement and that he, Paul, told Peter that he was wrong. Probably if Paul had known that he was writing Scripture, he would have toned down his remarks. But Paul was writing a letter to Christians in Galatia. Isn't it common for us when writing to someone we know and care deeply about to cut the diplomacy and tell them straight out our opinions and views? Paul reported in Galatians about a conflict that he and Peter had in Antioch. Apparently the reason for Paul reporting this incident was to help the Christians in Galatia experience the grace of God and be agents of grace to others.

One of the first issues to arise for the early church was whether followers of Christ who were Gentiles had to become Jews in order to be Christians. Peter dealt with that issue with Cornelius and that incident became the model for the church to follow. Once a person experiences liberation in one area of life, he or she begins to be liberated in others. When Peter crossed the threshold of accepting Cornelius, he also crossed the threshold of eating with Gentiles. Peter was comfortable with this position until some of the leaders from Jerusalem came to see him. They intimidated Peter by their presence and concern about this issue, and Peter changed his position. Several others followed Peter's lead. Paul was very upset with Peter and told Peter to his face in Antioch that he was wrong.

One of the hazards of being in a leadership position is that it is practically impossible to act privately. Whatever is done is viewed, observed, analyzed, and evaluated. This was certainly true with Peter. Whether or not it was really wise of Paul to make a public spectacle of Peter's actions is worth reviewing.

Some anonymous person gave every minister some sound advice: "Sin, like any sore, needs to be exposed. But preachers don't need to do it with a broad axe; usually just a pin prick in the right place does the trick."

Paul's action was more like a broad axe than a pin prick. He confronted Peter for having acted insincerely; having "played the hypocrite" is more the meaning of the phrase.

A critical issue at stake in all of this from Paul's perspective was the temptation for the followers of Christ to get into rule making and rule keeping. Paul knew the dead end to which legalism led. He knew from personal experience there was no life in that approach. As difficult as it had been for him, his encounter with Christ had transformed him. He had been converted from a strict adherent to the letter of the law, religious rule keeping, to one basking in the freedom of grace. There were times when his old rigidity surfaced, as when he sent John Mark home from a trip with him and as here in his rather brash and harsh treatment of Peter and Barnabas. He was upset that Barnabas had gone along with Peter, and there is no indication that Paul and Barnabas ever traveled together after this. Remember after Paul's experience on the Damascus road when no one trusted him, that it was Barnabas who stood up for him and encouraged the followers of the Way to take a chance on him. Paul never quite developed the sensitivity that Barnabas had.

In Paul's defense, he was concerned that the movement would take a giant step backwards into legalism. Personified in Peter's action was Paul's worst fear. Paul was fearful that people would start thinking that their relationship with God was dependent on works of the law, which designates any religious system whose hope for acceptance by God rests upon obeying rules. Paul had discovered through Christ that God wants to relate, love, and care for people just because that is God's nature—all people, Jews and Gentiles alike. Not only are people not obligated to earn God's love and favor, but it is impossible to do and impossible to maintain. If our relationship with God were based on merit, no one would ever relate to God. A relationship based on merit becomes narrower and increasingly restrictive. A relationship based on grace always is growing and expanding.

The trap that Paul sought to help the Galatians avoid was not a new one, and the trap was not removed once and for all with Paul's strong appeal. People trough the centuries have gotten caught up in rigidity, rule keeping, and legalism. Many centuries after Paul, Martin Luther discovered that he was attempting to win God's favor by defining all of life in clearly black and white terms. Luther was a monk who obeyed every rule of his religious order. Finally he became so stressed out that he discovered God was graceful toward him and accepted him. Luther learned the importance of being saved by faith through grace. Later, Luther summarized his attempts to earn God's favor and love by saying, "If ever a man could be saved by monkery that man was I."

What Luther discovered was grace. What Paul discovered was grace. What he saw Peter reverting to was religious rule keeping. That approach nullifies everything that God sought to accomplish through the total event of Christ's life. Too often, as far as we are concerned, Christ lived for no purpose, died for no purpose, and was resurrected for no purpose because his life makes no difference in our living. As far as we are concerned Jesus' entire experience was a waste. But God took the chance anyway, hoping we would open ourselves to graceful love and acceptance.

A large ship was at sea. Suddenly, a blip appeared on the radar screen. "Tell that ship to change its course fifteen degrees!" said the captain. The radio man did, and the word came back on the radio, "*You* change *your* course fifteen degrees." "Tell that ship that we're in the right and to change its course fifteen degrees," said the captain. The radio man did as he was told, and the word came back again, "You change your course fifteen degrees." This time the captain himself got on the radio and said, "I am the captain. Change your course fifteen degrees." The word came back over the radio: "You change your course fifteen degrees. I am a lighthouse!"

Isn't there a sense in which we live our lives on a collision course with the way of God? We become enamored with the two or three good deeds we have done. We plow through the sea of life, and when the signal of God's grace appears on the radar screen, either we don't recognize it or we expect it to adjust to our course.

Paul stated clearly in his letter to the Galatian Christians that God's grace is shining to give light and rescue all who will respond. To ignore God's grace or to refuse to accept God's grace is to nullify the grace of God.

Grace has been defined as "the love of God, spontaneous, beautiful, unearned, at work in Jesus Christ for the salvation of people" (A. M. Hunter, *Interpreting the Parables*). This is the theology of the gospel. To be true to that gospel, Jesus had to hold fast to the point of opening God's kingdom to publicans and prostitutes. He couldn't move aside on this issue even for the oncoming good, moral, religious people who demanded a slight alteration of course.

Karl Barth said that every sermon should begin by speaking of grace. Only after grace is experienced can anyone be open enough to God to do any genuine repenting. Too often we reverse the sequence, holding back grace as if it were a bit of candy offered to a child only after the child takes a bad-tasting medicine of repentance.

The Andy Capp comic strip illustrates the difficulty of grace that forgiveness expresses. There is a minister whom Andy dodges all the time, because Andy is always in the bar and never in church. One day Flo, Andy's wife, for the umpteenth time, decides to take Andy back home again. The minister commends Flo saying, "Flo, I'm so glad you took him back again." And Flo says, "There's something about me; I just have to forgive and forget." Under his breath, Andy says, "There's something about her, all right. She never forgets that she forgives."

Many of us are like Flo. We forgive, but like Peter we wonder how many times we should forgive someone. Seven times? If we keep a record of how many times we have forgiven someone, we really haven't forgiven them. We haven't received grace, and we have not been graceful toward others.

Another attitude that gets in the way of grace is resentment. There are people who don't keep forgiveness records because they are resenting what another person has done. To resent means to feel again. To hang on to our hurt feelings that someone else has caused us blocks the flow of grace to us, and thus grace cannot flow through us to others. The best way I know to understand grace is in terms of unconditional love. God loves the world, loves you and me with no strings attached. God loves us and desperately wants us to love in return, but whether we love God or anyone, God will continue to love us.

There is a moving dialogue in Lorraine Hansberry's play *A Raisin in the Sun*. The plot concerns a poor black family. The father has died, and the family is awaiting the $10,000 from the life insurance policy. The mother wants to use part of the money to make a down payment on a house and the rest of the money to help with her daughter's college education. The daughter wants to become a doctor. The son wants to invest the money in a liquor store where they can get rich quick. The mother gives the money to the son to put in the bank for safe keeping until they can find the house they want. The son gives the money to an acquaintance to invest in the liquor store. The acquaintance skips town with the money.

After a heated argument with her mother, the daughter cries out: "be on my side for once! You saw what he did. . . . Wasn't it you who taught me . . . to despise any man who would do that?" The mother answers: "Yes—I taught you that. Me and your daddy. But I taught you something else, too. . . . I thought I taught you to love him." "Love him," the daughter screams. "There's nothing left to love."

Then the mother utters these memorable lines:

There is always something left to love. And if you ain't learned that, you ain't learned nothing. Have you cried for that boy today? I don't mean for yourself and for the family 'cause we lost the money. I mean for him; what he been through and what it done to him. Child, when you think is the time to love somebody the most; when they done good and made things easy for everybody? Well then, you ain't through learning—because that ain't the time at all. It's when he's at his lowest and can't believe in hisself 'cause the world done whipped him so. When you starts measuring somebody, measure him right, child, measure him right. Make sure you done taken into account what hills and valleys he come through before he got to wherever he is."

In our situations, God always takes into account the hills and the valleys we've come through to get wherever we are. That is grace and love all rolled into relationship with God. We can be assured that God will be faithful to the relationship, will be faithful to loving us and responding to us with grace. We can see and experience God's loving and graceful faithfulness most clearly in Jesus of Nazareth. As we seek to emulate Christ's kind of love and grace in our relationships, we are crucified with Christ. Then, it is no longer we who live, but Christ lives in us and through us, communicating the grace of God to every person we meet. Any attempt to draw up rules, regulations, and religious hoops that people must jump through to receive God's love or to demonstrate they are deserving of grace is to declare Jesus' life null and void. Let us celebrate the grace of God that has freely been offered to us. And let us be assured that God always takes into account the hills and valleys we have come through to get wherever we are. That is the grace of God's faithfulness to us.

Finding Stillness in a Turning World

Galatians 2:17-20

Charles B. Bugg

In a poem T. S. Eliot speaks of "the still point in a turning world." How do we find something that gives us equilibrium in a convulsively changing world?

Paul wrote to the Galatians, and he shared with them the "still point" in his changing world. "I have been crucified with Christ, and I no longer live but Christ lives in me," the apostle wrote. Paul was writing into the teeth of a major crisis. The churches of Galatia were struggling to balance the issues of law and grace. They had come under the influence of a Jewish background. For people influenced by Judaism, the Torah, the law of Moses, had been central. It was the glue that held them together.

Paul had come with the message of grace. It wasn't that Paul was trying to abolish the law, but the emphasis of his preaching presented a dilemma. "How," his listeners asked, "do we receive this grace and at the same time not desert the law that has been so critical to our faith?"

That kind of struggle is always difficult. The call to faith is the call to let go of something old in order to cling to something new. It's the age-old dilemma of leaving and cleaving. A minister stands in front of a couple at a wedding ceremony and speaks glibly about the need to leave and cleave. If the minister thinks about it, however, he or she knows how difficult it is to do that. Besides, we ministers really don't mean for this young couple to leave completely their parents, their family, or their history. As a minister, I would not feel good if the bride told me after the wedding, "I just told my Mom good-bye. I'll never see her again. You did say to leave, didn't you?"

What we are talking about is a tension, the right balance of things. Law is important. None of us would want to live in a society with no laws. Neither did Jesus mean that the invitation to follow him was an invitation to follow our own impulses. Grace is not the door that leads to the land of everybody doing his or her own thing.

Grace does, however, mean freedom and faith to follow someone as the center of our lives and not just to follow some rules. That was Paul's message. He wanted the Galatians to understand that the Torah has now taken shape in the person of Jesus the Christ. What that means is of fundamental importance; what counts is not rules or regulations but relationship to the Christ. Out of that relationship comes our obedience.

So Paul spoke to the issue of what justifies us or makes us right with God. Then he moved from that issue to the issue of himself. What was it that was central to *his* life? What had *he* discovered that was "the still point in his turning world?"

He began by speaking of something that had died. There had been a funeral in Paul's life: "I have been crucified with Christ, and I no longer live. . . ." What in the world did Paul mean? Something so big, so shattering had happened to him that he said, "I no longer live. . . ."

When I was a student in college, I gave up dancing for a year. I would sit at the parties at the fraternity house, snap my finger, tap my toes, and sing along with the music; but for a year, I did not dance. In my younger days, dancing was one of those things that separated the "ordinary" saints from the "super" saints. I had begun to preach in some youth revivals. I had some success, and some people told me that if I was really committed, I could probably be a well-known preacher one day. So, in a convoluted twist of logic,

I decided that if I gave up dancing, God would reward me by making me a famous preacher.

I look back with some embarrassment. Not only did I miss a year of dancing, but also I was doing it to achieve fame. Is that the kind of thing Paul meant when he said: "I have been crucified with Christ, and I no longer live"? At that time, I would have said yes. Now I hardly think so. Paul was plunging much deeper than whether we dance, play cards, or go to a movie on Sunday. In his own life, Paul the pre-Christian had exemplified what it means to be good. Few had accomplished what he had. Even fewer had the fervor that he had for his faith. Why, when he was converted to Christ, he was on his way to do more damage to that pesky Nazarene sect!

What Paul found on the road to Damascus was that his goodness was not good enough. In fact, his desire to be so good had turned into evil. He could persecute people who disagreed with him without flinching. Because he was good and right, the old Paul felt that he could decide what was good and right for everybody else.

Is that a problem in our time? Look around. How many people have been hurt by folks who felt they were good and right and who wanted to make sure that everyone else was good and right. When our goodness is front and center, evil things can happen. Tolerance is sacrificed, people are killed either by the sword or by words, and all of it is done in the name of the God who is on our side.

We should never forget that Paul was good before he met the grace of God. He wasn't some rough-looking character staggering of the bus. He was as good as he knew how to be, and that was his danger. Goodness is not enough. So Paul had a funeral, and he said, "I no longer live. . . ."

That's not the end of the story. Something new came alive: "But Christ lives in me." The conjunction, "but," is a contrast, not a continuation. Something radical happened. Something revolutionary. He met the grace of God and knew that the center of life had become Christ. Saul had always been doing something. Paul then realized that God had done something for him, and that was the center out of which he came to live.

Did that mean that Paul abandoned all the laws? No. Look at his life. He exemplified obedience. But he was not good in order to get God's favor; he was good because God's favoring grace lived in Paul and through Paul. No longer did Paul have to make other people good and right. He could finally preach with passion and trust the God who had changed his life.

Do you see the difference before Damascus and after? Before he was good, but he was dangerous. Compulsively he tried to convert everyone to his side. It had to be his way or no way.

What we see in Paul is the picture of a person living out of the stormy desperation to be so good. One day, however, that person was found by the grace of God. That person still lived in a "turning world." There was a big difference, though. I would call it a security, an identity, a stillness. Whatever you may choose to call it, we would all agree that it's a work of God's grace.

The Crisis of Blessing and Faith

Galatians 3:6-14

Vaughn CroweTipton

When was the last time someone you knew and trusted, turned out to be something very different than you expected? Many of us have experienced the pain and anger of realizing our trust has been abused or misplaced by someone important to us. If you have never experienced this kind of pain, hold on. Your day is probably coming. People being what they are, our lives being the way they are, and most importantly, our expectations being what they are, hold on, your day is coming. While our nature typically causes us to resolve that scenario negatively, maybe for you that something different turned out to be something very good. Perhaps that person in your life exceeded all your expectations, and you now can proudly say "I knew her when . . ." or "Who would have thought good ol' what's his name would have gotten so far?"

For many of us, change and all the experiences that surround it, especially in relationships, are difficult. When people who are important to us become more or less than we expect, our relationship with them changes, sometimes for better and sometimes for worse. When things don't fit as neatly into our world as we think they should, or as they once did, we again face possibility of change. We struggle and often find ourselves in crisis. We all encounter these crucial points in our relationships. It is an experience universal to being human.

As we will see, the Galatians were about to be in crisis. Their day had definitely come. Things were no longer going to fit neatly for them and certainly their relationships were about to change. Paul, who was never one for easing someone into a new situation, minced no words as he attempted to remind them of the gospel they had left behind so easily. Imagine receiving Paul's letter and reading his stinging words: "You foolish Galatians!" No doubt about it, the nature of their relationship with each other and more importantly, with God was about to change. No doubt about it, they had a real crisis on their hands.

Their crisis actually started when some of the Galatians began listening to some Judaizing Christians. They were trying to convince the Galatians that following Christ was not enough. They were being told and were beginning to be convinced that living under Jewish Law and circumcision were necessary for salvation. The unspoken message in that teaching was that those who were not willing to follow those practices were excluded. For the Jews, it was a believable message—they were circumcised, and they had followed the Law all their lives. For the Gentiles, the message was problematic.

Paul wrote to remind all of them that there was no other gospel, no other truth, than the one he preached—salvation comes through faith in Christ. This gospel, he argued, comes from God. In chapter two of his letter (2:11-14), Paul recalled for his readers a time when Peter wavered in similar circumstances. What Paul said in effect to Peter, he now stated plainly to the Galatians: "If justification comes through the Law, then Christ died for nothing" (2:21). The crisis had begun. Giving up on old inadequate beliefs is never easy for anyone. Crises of faith are often painful and nearly always involve one of two things: a process of rebuilding or rejection.

The Chinese have an interesting perspective on crisis. Their character for crisis is made up of two symbols. The first means danger. Most of the time, we perceive crisis in this way. An event changes what is normal and comfortable for us, so we react strongly and struggle to hold on to what is secure. When we perceive danger in our lives, we tend to retreat or fight. In faith crises, neither option is healthy. Our faith, in order to be vibrant and strong, needs to be continually challenged. An athlete who never faces a challenge will never grow or find that hidden potential. People who stagnate in their faith, likewise, never grow or find that hidden potential. When the crisis does come, and for all of us that day will come, they are unprepared to deal with it appropriately.

The second symbol of the Chinese character means opportunity. When a crisis, especially a faith crisis, is viewed from this perspective, there are innumerable possibilities, the greatest of which is the potential for growth.

Paul's opponents in Galatia, like those Peter faced, had their own expectations of how God works. Don't we all? For many of us, we learn these expectations from our experiences in church and with each other. What we need is to learn to base our expectations of God on Scripture. Paul's message to the Galatians and the word for us today is that God is not limited by our expectations or our prejudices. We all have expectations of God that are not met, and many of those expectations have no basis in Scripture. Even those who should have known Jesus best struggled with unmet expectations. In the opening chapter of Acts the disciples stand with the resurrected Christ just before his ascension and ask, after all they had been taught about the kingdom, "Lord, is it at this time when you will restore the kingdom to Israel?" (Acts 1:6). Their expectations of the kingdom and God were set on what *they* thought should be, not on what Jesus had taught them. I can't help but imagine a frustrated Jesus sighing in disbelief and wondering if his disciples would ever understand. They did come to understand, however, and the book of Acts portrays a wonderful story of how the gospel spread unhindered beyond all kinds of prejudicial boundaries.

Paul's opponents expected new converts to live under the Law as Jews. Author J. B. Phillips would have responded to those opponents, "Your God is too small."[1] Their view of how God works in the world placed boundaries around what God could do and with whom God could work. Their God simply wasn't *big* enough to get over the boundary of the Law.

But let's not hastily point our fingers at Paul's opponents. Their point of view was based in Scripture. In Genesis 15 God said to Abraham: "Look toward heaven and count the stars if you are able to count them. . . . So shall your descendants be" (15:6). God also promised Abraham land: "I am the Lord who brought you from Ur of the Chaldeans, to give you this land to possess" (15:7). God had made promises to Abraham, and for God to be faithful, those promises had to be kept. The problem between Paul and his opponents was, to whom did these promises belong? For the opponents, the promises belonged only to Israel and those who would follow Israel's Law. For Paul, the promises belonged to anyone willing to follow God. That's why Paul quoted Genesis 15:6: "Abraham believed God, and it was reckoned to him as righteousness" (Gal 15:6). Paul used this quotation to show that Abraham and his descendants never were saved by keeping the Law. Their salvation, as our salvation, came through faith and faith alone. Therefore, anyone who believes becomes a child of Abraham.

What Paul created for those opponents was a crisis of definition. Their religious world was defined by who they believed they were in the eyes of God, descendants of Abraham. Paul's argument in this letter was that following the law does not make anyone a descendant of Abraham.

You probably know that defining your role in a relationship is never easy, and once the relationship is defined, human nature drives us to hang onto it as it is. We like security. Our tendency, and this was the sin of the opponents, is to exclude others once certain walls of definition are erected. Definitions are naturally exclusive. They bracket out what does not fit the definition. The problem is that when we define God, or God's expectations too narrowly, we put God in an inadequate box.

The Talmud contains a story about Abraham and his box for God. Abraham invited an elderly man to his tent to join him in prayer to the one spiritual God. Learning that the man was a fire-worshiper, Abraham drove the man from his door. That night God appeared to Abraham in a vision and said: "I have borne with that ignorant man for seventy years; could you not have patiently suffered with him one night?" When our boxes that explain God or our expectations of God are inadequate, we leave out too much or try to include more than is possible.

For example, too often people believe that if they simply live a good life, then God's response will be to give great and good things to them. This kind of definition puts God in the position of being a job performance supervisor, handing out increases to the industrious workers and cuts to the slack workers. This kind of definition excludes reality. Many good people have bad things happen to them. Not because of what they've done or because God is displeased with them or their performance. Bad things happen in this world of free choice. The writer of Ecclesiates said: "In my vain life I have seen everything; there are righteous people who perish in their righteousness and there are wicked people who prolong their life in evildoing" (7:15). Any understanding of how God interacts with us must be wide enough to account for the reality of the world in which we live. Otherwise, parts of God's creation, individual human beings, are left outside of God's grace. Imagine the terrible guilt of feeling as if you have let your family down because you weren't good enough for God and now your family is suffering. Bad things do happen to good people. And we all know too many stories of how less than virtuous individuals prosper, despite their relationship to God. God doesn't pass out good or bad things on the basis of merit. The reality is life is hard. More important is this reality: God is good and does pass out grace, not for what we have done, but because that's who God is.

Paul's opponents tried to place a burden on the Gentiles even ancient Israel could not bear. They placed both God and the Gentiles in boxes that were inadequate. Their expectations were too small for God and too grand for the Gentiles. Israel's own history in the book of Judges indicates that it could not keep the Law. Over and over again, Israel fell into sin, judgement, and exile only to be brought back by God's grace. Paul said: "For this reason, those who believe are blessed with Abraham who believed" (3:9). Because ancient Israel had failed to keep the Law, the nation suffered the consequences of its curse: "For all who rely on the works of the Law are under a curse" (3:10). Therefore, to try to do what was required of ancient Israel was to join with it in that curse. Paul concluded, therefore, that "it is evident that no one is justified before God by the Law; for the one who is righteous will live by faith" (3:11).

The fact is we all fall short and need something greater than ourselves to pull us up out of the depths that life throws us into. What Paul's letter tells us is that nothing outside of God's grace can do that for us. If we don't account for the vast grace of God, our God will be too small. Anytime we leave out God's grace, we leave out certain people and our definitions and expectations are inadequate. It is only God's grace that is sufficient to save Abraham and his children, both ancient and modern.

Paul's message contained difficult words for his opponents to hear. He has used their own Scriptures to show how their previous position was inadequate. He had also clearly challenged their view of God. The crisis that they faced was an important one and one that we face as well. How do we think about God, talk about God, and relate to God without limiting God at the same time? We need to ask ourselves how we limit God in our lives and the lives of other people. There are at least three positive things important for us to remember as we struggle with these issues. Paul provided these as examples for us.

First, any answer we have for these questions should be biblical. Paul gave us a clear example in his use of Scripture. For all the searching we do in our language to find some way to understand God, Scripture gives us more help than we can imagine. Like a child playing hide and seek who wants to be found but realizes the hiding place is too secure, a finger or a foot appears in plain sight giving away the secret. God is like that in Scripture. We could never have found or defined God on our own, but we don't have to because God has done it for us.

Second, we must all admit to ourselves that change is inevitable. That's not to say we can expect God to be changing all the time. The fact is we change. Our experiences add up to new perspectives, different views, and fresh insights. Who we are from day to day is never the same. Advice given to me by an older friend not long before I was married has always stayed with me. He said, "Remember that you can never stay in love with the woman you married, you need to love the woman you are married to." We all change. We are all potential waiting to happen. Buried in each of us is all the people we have not yet become, but might be someday. If we try to remain the person we were years ago or are today, if we ask our friends and spouses to remain the same person we always knew, we do them and ourselves a great disservice. Change and growth go hand in hand, and without them we stagnate and die.

Many people, however, refuse to accept change. Their concept of God remains the same as it was the first time they encountered their Lord. What they miss out on by remaining in this state of denial is a fresh and vital relationship with a God who cares about them and wants them to become all they were intended to be. Paul's opponents fit into this category. Holding desperately on to the past, they missed the presence of God among humanity in Christ Jesus.

Finally, we must realize that we are all recipients of God's grace. Even Israel, who could not keep the convenant and remain faithful, received God's grace time after time. That is the true message of the gospel. Christ came and redeemed us and was cursed for us so that "the blessing of Abraham might come to" all of us "so that we might receive the promise of the Spirit through faith" (3:14). Faith is the most appropriate response to this gift, and in such faith lies our greatest freedom and hope.

Listen to this true story. A young pastor who was concerned with his own search for growth and meaning was trying to prepare his Sunday sermon. As he wrestled with it, he had a dream that he was entering the front of the church in order to move down the aisle to the pulpit. He noticed on his way in that he didn't have a shirt and tie, but someone gave these to him as he entered. He put them on and went to the pulpit, delivering the most powerful sermon he had ever delivered. When Sunday came, his dream came true, at least the part about delivering his most powerful sermon ever.

When he related this story to a friend, the friend asked, "What do you think the dream meant?" This young pastor said that as long as he kept his own personal expectations and prejudices inside, there was never enough clothing to cover him. On other occasions, he had dreamed that his clothing was too tight. When he unloaded his burden, there was enough clothing to take care of his nakedness. Like everyone else, he had to be exposed before he could be clothed, to be open before he could receive affirmation.[2]

Grace is a covering. It is that which makes us adequate when we would otherwise be exposed. What clothing is to the body, grace is to the spirit. Grace is what the law can never be. The death of Christ removes the curse brought about by the breaking of the law. The covenant promises made with Abraham are renewed by God's grace, the sign of membership in those promises is faith, and nothing can limit that.

Notes

[1]J. B. Phillips, *Your God is too Small* (New York: the Macmillan Company, 1961).

[2]Adapted from *Faith at Work*, August (1977), 19.

Beyond the Burden
of Being Good

Galatians 3:20

Gregory L. Hunt

I have been crucified with Christ. Nevertheless, I live; yet, not I, but Christ lives in me; and the life I now live I live by faith in the Son of God, who loved me and gave his life for me. Galatians 3:20

As a boy growing up in the home of "salt-of-the-earth" Baptists, I always looked forward to revival services. We could count on having a guest preacher or song leader with a gripping testimony. I confess that what I liked most about their testimonies was not how Christ had changed them; what I liked most was their description of the kind of life they had led before their conversion. Their pre-Christian experience always seemed more interesting than the life they now were leading. I envied them their past and regretted that I had become a child of the church before I could develop a good testimony of my own!

I offer this confession not to cleanse my conscience but to confront that tendency in each of us to equate Christian commitment with "behaving ourselves" (by which we mean doing without most of the things we really enjoy). This is the view of the Christian life that made me jealous of "honest-to-goodness sinners." It is a vision of life that often takes form in the imaginations of high-energy, school-aged boys and girls who are being forced to dress up in

Sunday clothes and sit still in church. No wonder so many people today are "voting with their feet" against organized religion. They are looking for life, not living death! They want freedom, not chains. The amazing thing is not that so many are leaving the traditional church, but that so many are staying, given their grim understanding of the life of denial it represents.

The language of the gospel can work against us here, if we take it to mean what some people suggest. The language of "the cross" —the language of "dying to self and living for God"—sounds for all the world like giving up on fun for the sake of faith when explained by the prim and proper. The cross becomes an anvil on the shoulders, a heavy weight of thankless service to be borne without complaint. Based on this version of discipleship, many of those who believe in heaven and hell secretly hope they can put off "giving their lives to Christ" until just before they die. The thought of trading in their freedom too soon makes them shudder.

We can be glad to know that when the Apostle Paul said "I have been crucified with Christ," he *was not* spitting out sour sentiment through pursed lips. He was describing with joy a kind of dying that leads to life. He was describing an escape hatch from the smothering tomb of legalism and sin; an escape hatch that opens into the fresh, clean air of a new and good life.

Paul spoke from the heart, as one who knew from firsthand experience how a person suffers when cut off from God. Spend a little time with people who feel smothered by the lives they have chosen, who now confess that they forgot to read the fine print on their contract with sin. Examine your own heart and the scar tissue from your sinful past that may even now be clogging the arteries of your joy. Sin does not advertise the pain that follows its pleasures. It promotes the succulence of that first bite rather than the bitter aftertaste that lingers.

To find oneself caught in the trap of temptation is to long for a way of escape. A seventh-grade girl who was having trouble with friends because of some things she had said confessed, "There are times I wish I were dead! Don't worry, I'm not going to commit suicide. I just wish I could move to somewhere new where no one knew me and start all over again!"

The gospel of the cross, according to Paul, is something like a place for starting all over again. When he said "I have been crucified with Christ," he was expressing the relief of someone who, having reaped a whirlwind of trouble as the master of his own life, reaches the point where he is ready—eager—to gather up his sin-weary bones and drag them to Calvary. The first step in discovering the joy of the cross is to wake up to the fact that the cross is God's answer to the seemingly inescapable trouble we bring on ourselves when we take charge of our lives. The cross gives us a way, figuratively speaking, to "die"—to put an unbearable life behind us.

We make an exhilarating discovery when we take recourse in the cross. We discover that giving into God does not mean the death of life, but life's fresh rebirth. "I have been crucified with Christ," Paul began, but then he continued, "Nevertheless, I live!"

To claim the gift of the cross is to find oneself cut loose from the prison of the unchangeable past. It is to find oneself forgiven, scrubbed clean, guilt-free. The life of sin forces us to live our lives under the cover of darkness. By way of the cross, we gain free passage back into the light of day. The point of the cross is not to kill us, but to do away with what *is* killing us so that we can truly live. Having been "crucified with Christ," we "live!"

Right here, right when things are looking up, many a Christian shipwrecks on the shores of legalism. Having been justified by the grace of God through faith, we think we must achieve perfection through the law. The way we fall back under the law can take any number of forms.

Some of us fall back under the law by linking our profession of faith with a religion of "do's and don'ts." Ask many persons in the church how to become a Christian, and they can tell you plainly and simply that it amounts to receiving the grace of God in Christ through faith. Ask them what it means to *be* a Christian, and they will say, "It means to live a good life." Salvation by grace through faith; life after salvation by strict adherence to a codebook on behavior. "Read your Bible, love your neighbor, pray to God, do not cuss or cheat or smoke or drink. Do not have fun; it is probably wrong."

For others, religious ritual is their way back under the tyranny of the law. Like those who brought their peace offerings to the temple in Jerusalem, many Christians think that faithful attendance at church and regular giving assure them their place in the Lamb's Book of Life. Severing Sunday from the other six days of the week, they develop religious routines that have nothing to do with the rest of their lives. Formalism replaces faith.

The most subtle way we fall back under the law is through the rat race of achievement. Having been saved by grace through faith, we live as though we still have something to prove—to God, to others, to ourselves. Having been justified by the power of God, we keep on with our pathetic efforts to succeed in our own strength.

Reflecting on Christian experience outside the strength of God, the Quaker mystic, Thomas Kelly, had this to say:

> Our lives in a modern city grow too complex and overcrowded. Even the necessary obligations which we feel we must meet grow overnight, like Jack's beanstalk, and before we know it we are bowed down with burdens, crushed under committees, strained, breathless, and hurried, panting through a never-ending program of appointments, . . . we're weary and breathless. And we know and regret that our life is slipping away, with our having tasted so little of the peace and joy and serenity we are persuaded it should yield to a soul of wide caliber.[1]

In this frustrating life under the law, we can identify with the apostle Paul who finally cried out in despair: "Wretched man that I am! Who will set me free from this body of death?" (Romans 7:24). Like captives of ancient conquerors whose punishment in defeat was to carry the corpse of a comrade strapped to their backs, so we, with Paul, suffer under the deadly weight and unbearable stench of the law!

Oh, to be free of this! What is needed is more than religious reform: getting right with God so you can go back to doing life in your own power. The gospel offers a better way, a way out of oppressive moralism, meaningless religious ritual, and the rat race of achievement with its frustation and burnout. The gospel offers a way to recreate life on entirely new foundations.

When we come to Christ by way of the cross, we are asking him to take over. The old self gets buried. In its place, Christ comes, entering our lives to reign within. We can quit trying to be good! The strain is not worth it. Nor is it necessary. Christ simply asks us to yield our lives to him, trusting that he will provide the goodness. This is how Paul put it: "Not I, but Christ lives in me."

After years of frustration trying to be good enough, John Wimber, the founder of the Vineyard Christian Fellowship, fell to his knees one morning in desperation and asked God to help him. The encounter that morning became a transforming moment in his life:

> I sensed God respond with these words: "The issue is not being good, it is being God's. Just come to me, and I will provide goodness for you." God explained that he had good works for me, but that they were his works, and I could not do them for him. He told me that I needed to begin to listen to his voice rather than try to distill the Christian life down to a set of rules and principles. This translated into more listening during prayer and Bible study; more conversation during the normal activities of the day. Then something interesting began to happen. God put new desires and attitudes in me. I experienced more of the Spirit's strength to act in ways that brought God joy. God's daily guidance became clearer and clearer. Not my good works, but God's good works, began to multiply in my life.[2]

Let us quickly add that the idea of "Christ coming into our lives to direct us" does not mean that we are mere empty vessels waiting to be filled. Selfhood is not destroyed in this process, rather it is transformed. We come under new management. We find ourselves animated by a new power: the Holy Spirit. When we open our lives to Christ, we realize our own unique potential by letting the power of God live in us and through us.

That, in fact, is what Paul had in mind when he said, "The life I now live in the flesh I live by faith." Life in Christ involves a radical yielding of self in obedient trust. The acrostic for "F.A.I.T.H." that I learned in a college discipleship program still puts it well: "*F*orsaking *A*ll, *I T*rust *H*im." After reading Galatians 3:20, one young Christian wrote these words in the margin: "I need to ease up and simply let Christ dwell in me."

Never fear what it might mean to give in to Christ. When we give in to Christ, says Paul, we give in to the one "who loved us and delivered himself up for us." How different this Lord is from any other would-be ruler of our lives. Those who want power tend to use that power for their own benefit. They want to gain mastery over us for their own ends. They use us and abuse us. Not so with Christ. He is motivated by self-giving love. By his own stated intent his goal has always been that we "might have life, and that more abundantly" (John 10:10). What was it he said when calling the crowds to follow?

> Come to me, all you that are weary and are carrying heavy burdens, and I will give you rest. Take my yoke upon you, and learn from me; for I am gentle and humble in heart, and you will find rest for your souls. For my yoke is easy, and my burden is light. (Matt 11:28-30)

Christ wants complete, undivided loyalty so that he can accomplish for us and through us what we never could ourselves.

A lot has happened in my life since those childhood days when I sat on the edge of the pew listening with rapt attention to tales of sin and salvation. I am better acquainted now with the grief of sin. I have a better understanding now of the discouragement that comes from relying too heavily on my own strength and wisdom. And by the grace of God I am finding for myself that the apostle Paul knew what he was talking about! There is life in the cross. There is freedom in following Jesus. There is power in yielding control to the one whose strength molded the mountains and still molds us in the name of love.

Hear Paul say it again. His words can become our own, personally realized day by day: "I have been crucified with Christ. Nevertheless, I live; yet, not I, but Christ lives in me; and the life I now live I live by faith in the Son of God, who loved me and gave his life for me."

Notes

[1]Thomas Kelly, *A Testament of Devotion* (San Francisco: Harper & Row, 1941) 102.

[2]John Wimber and Kevin Springer, *Power Evangelism* (San Francisco: Harper Collins, 1992) 42.

Does It Fit?

Galatians 3:23-29

William L. Turner

The man who wrote *The Last Temptation of Christ* and *Zorba the Greek*, Nikos Kazantzakis, has another novel entitled *The Greek Passion* in which he tells of a small Greek village that annually produced a play depicting the passion of Christ. The cast is selected a year in advance, and as the story unfolds, the lives of those chosen begin to take on the characteristics of those whom they are to portray. Strangely enough, the man chosen to play Judas Iscariot begins to act like Judas; the man chosen to portray Simon Peter acts much like Simon; and the man chosen to play Jesus ends up being killed by a group of his fellow townspeople.

Identity is a strange and wonderful thing. We are born with it; some of it comes with our genes. Then they give us an identity at the hospital. But we also choose one for ourselves later on. Many who attend church have chosen "Christian believer" as an important part of their identity.

Paul described that choice in his letter to the Galatians as something we are "baptized into," something we have "put on" as one would put on clothing. In doing so, Paul stood squarely in the tradition of much ancient thought. In ancient mystery religions, for instance, one might be initiated into the cult by putting on a robe that was symbolic of the character, dignity, and power of the god with which one wanted to identify. Also, one of the initiatory rites of Judaism was baptism (along with circumcision and sacrifice in the temple)—"and this was called being baptized into Judaism." The early Christians carried this practice over into their new religion and sometimes clothed their converts in white robes to symbolize their having been "baptized into Christ."

But does it fit?

There's the rub!

That has kept a lot of people from ever becoming followers of Christ. "I can't be like that. I can't live up to this or that," they say. Such feelings are based on a misunderstanding of Christian faith.

But when we *have* chosen Christ as Lord, when we have "clothed ourselves" in him, what may we expect? Some of us have worn the clothes of Christ longer than others, but all of us are still trying to make them fit. What should we look for to determine if they are fitting well? Paul gives us a few good ideas right here in Galatians 3.

The Beginning of a Journey

One who puts on Christ can expect to begin a journey. Paul depicted the situation this way:

> Therefore the law was our disciplinarian until Christ came, so that we might be justified by faith. But now that faith has come, we are no longer subject to a disciplinarian. For in Christ Jesus you are all children of God through faith. (Gal 4:24-26)

In Paul's mind, the law does basically two things. First, *it specifies our sin*—defining morality for us and holding things in check in society. Thus, it clearly shows us how far short we come in our sin.

Second, *it gets us ready for Christ*. The word Paul used here in verse 24 is *paidagogos*—a household slave who was the moral instructor of the family's children and who took them to school, leaving them with their teacher. The Law, said Paul, leads us as far as it can go and then turns us over to Christ. The Law can show us our need for salvation and forgiveness, but in order to meet that need, it leads us toward another, even Christ.

Therefore, when I come to put my faith in Christ, I embark on a whole new way of knowing and relating to God. The life of faith is *freedom*, not *legalism*. It is *experiential*, not *second-hand*. It is a *life in process*, not *static reality*. So, in "putting" on Jesus Christ, you can expect to begin a journey.

Now, spiritual growth is where you are headed, and that will not be quick or easy. Unfortunately, we have sometimes passed off our faith as an instant panacea for all ills, and we have drawn the sting of struggle. If Christianity is just a matter of "getting saved," then it does not matter what happens between conversion and heaven.

But Christianity is more than "getting saved," and the New Testament says that struggle does matter. Jesus said,"Follow me, and I will make you . . ." (Matt 4:19). Paul said, "And all of us, . . . are being transformed into the same image from one degree of glory unto another" (2 Cor 3:18). The writer of Second Peter urged all Christians to "grow in the grace and knowledge of our lord and savior Jesus Christ" (2 Pet 3:18). And, the First Epistle of John reminds us, "We are God's children now; what we will be has not yet been revealed" (1 John 3:2).

What does this mean? It means that my decision to follow Christ is a decision to let his Spirit overtake the drift of my life and begin reshaping it. This is not easy, for Christ does not "fit" me in many ways. The suit is too tight here or too loose there, and so on.

But the rest of the expectations are a lot easier if I accept the reality of this first one—that when I begin to follow Christ I begin the struggle toward maturity. This is built in. It's a given.

The Discovery of Personal Uniqueness

I have started on a journey, so now I can expect to know my own uniqueness. Paul said this:

> There is no longer Jew or Greek, there is no longer slave or free, there is no longer male or female; for all of you are one in Christ. (3:28)

This verse says that I won't any longer be a category or a stereotype. In Christ I'm a unique human being. You see, this new clothing, this Christianity, is *not* a uniform. It is not a uniform in which I lose my identity to march in step with every other Christian. It is clothing that is "tailor-made."

Paul was speaking here about an equality of status and a unity of purpose within the Christian community—but there is as much diversity in discipleship as there are persons in discipleship. And Paul gave attention to this in Romans and in his letters to the Corinthians when he talked about the multiplicity and diversity of spiritual gifts and qualities within the church.

So, becoming a Christian does not mean selling out my personhood! On the contrary, it may mean discovering it, affirming it, celebrating it. Personhood is a process, and Christianity is a way of affirming and enlarging that process.

Christianity is often misunderstood at this point. People see faith as the enemy of freedom, of independence, of personal uniqueness. C. S. Lewis used the analogy of salt in a helpful way here. He said that we should imagine a person who has never tasted salt. We give him some on the tip of his tongue, and his response would likely be: "That's strong, sharp, powerful stuff." We tell him that western cookery uses salt extensively, and his response might be: "In that case, I suppose all your dishes take exactly the same, because the taste of that stuff you have just given me is so strong that it will kill the taste of everything else." But, of course, just the opposite is true. Salt brings out the unique tastes of food when used properly. It does not negate them.[1] Just so, in a wonderful and mysterious way, the more I become Christ's person, the more I become my own, true person. And, my own unique qualities are blended into a fitting discipleship.

This, of course, does not just refer to the positive qualities. *All* of who you are—positive and negative—can nourish your growth as a Christian. Sin is not to be denied or evaded by the Christian. We are called to struggle against it, to confess it, and to learn from it. It is a part of our pilgrimage as human beings; it can be a boon to growth—provided we face it and own it and handle it with the help of Christ. As a Christian, expect to know your uniqueness.

The Acceptance of Other People

You can also expect to accept other people. This too is what Galatians 3:28 is about. Inside and outside the early church, there were Jewish extremists—people who felt that the only reason God created Gentiles was to fuel the fires of hell. There were also the Greek elitists—those who saw others as barbarians, obviously inferior to themselves. Jewish men often prayed a particular prayer in which they thanked God that they were not born *women.*

Paul was saying here that the phony walls between persons ought to go down. Agreed! But sometimes they don't. When they dont, the "suit" becomes uncomfortable. Sometimes our faith becomes a means of distance between us and others. Even in the body of Christ, we can become extremists or elitists.

This can happen when we only give "lip service" to our affirmation of personal uniqueness rather than "internalizing" it so that it affects our attitudes. If we *are* unique, and if Christ calls out that uniqueness into his service, he does not call with one voice! Of course, I would feel better sometimes if he did speak with one voice—my voice—and I imagine most persons have have similar feelings about their opinions. But Christ speaks to and through *all* his people. Thus, an important part of my struggle is to hear what he is saying through other persons. That is another way of talking about accepting another person.

This is a lifelong struggle, isn't it? I remember that years ago, after I—a white Southerner—had learned to begin accepting black people, some white people who were even harder to accept turned up! And when I—the product of a conservative Baptist church in the deep South—finally learned to accept "liberals" as Christians, up jumped some "fundamentalists" with whom I've really had to struggle.

Affirming and accepting the uniqueness of other persons (even when they are believers) is a continuous, often frustrating process. But it is a necessary part of a pilgrimage toward Christian maturity.

No one in our church family speaks for God exclusively (least of all, the pastor!). That is why acceptance and understanding of each other is a crucial struggle. Amazingly, however, when we do give ourselves to this kind of struggle, we learn to know each other. And when we know each other, we are better able to affirm and love each other—and that's becoming more like Christ! If you follow him, instead of perpetuating those old inequities of race or sex or standing, you can expect to begin accepting other people.

The Commitment of One's Life

Finally, I can expect to commit my life. Paul's words are very explicit about this: "For in Christ you *are* all children of God through faith" (3:26). I believe those words. I think it's very simple to feel that kind of thing deeply when faith is in embryo or infancy.

I did. I remember the first blush of personal commitment that I felt as a new Christian. As a boy who had just surrendered his life to Jesus Christ, I wanted to belong to him, to follow him, to serve him. I was ready! As Linus (of "Peanuts" fame) said: "In all this world there is nothing more inspiring than the sight of someone who has just been taken off the hook!" Forgiveness felt good to me, and Jesus Christ had my undying devotion.

But in adulthood, I have found that Christian commitment often isn't easy.

It would do us good, periodically, to stop and ask ourselves, "What or who am I *really* building my life on? Where is the actual base of my security?"

One of Paul Tournier's analogies is that the core reality of life is like a trapeze bar. It's what you are actually swinging from, what you're actually depending on to help you survive. What is it for you? In your mind (especially in your Sunday-morning mind) you may say, "It's Christ!" But is it? Is that your real source of security?

In my life, the trapeze is sometimes the approval of other people. Sometimes it is financial stability. Sometimes it's the need to succeed in my career. I find myself swinging from one of those bars to the others quite a bit!

But the test of my faith is when the bar of Christ swings into view. it may be in the form of social involvement, personal ministry, the investment of time or money, or giving myself to a relationship in order to share the good news of God's forgiveness. Now if I am willing to turn loose of the bar I'm holding and grab hold of the bar of Christ, I am taking a giant step toward authentic Christianity. It's only when I'm willing to risk going from other sources of security to Christ that I'm going to reach out for true freedom and genuine security.

And this, too, is a process.

Most of the time we swing back and forth. That's okay. We don't cease being disciples when we cease moving ahead. God doesn't stop loving us and calling us to pilgrimage when we stall and sputter on the road.

God just keeps loving us and calling us and urging us. God gives us a faith-family to travel with. Please notice that Paul's words here are full of plural nouns and pronouns—we, us, all of you, heirs, children. A great trapeze act is a group effort. In fact, it's usually a family act!

So, we struggle to become people who increasingly belong to Christ, peole with better fitting suits! "We've 'put on' Christ," said Paul. And so we have. But the joys and pains, the excitement and frustration of Christian discipleship are bound up, not in our beginnings, but in our struggles to become Christ's persons—in relationship to our own uniqueness, to one another, and to him.

Difficult? Demanding? Of course!

But we are not alone! That is one of the most beautiful parts of it. There is a Christ at our sides—in us and working through us to actualize a mature discipleship. And his example is before us to inspire us.

> Dear Master, in whose life I see
> All that I would, but fail to be.
> Let thy clear light forever shine,
> To shame and guide this life of mine.
>
> Though what I dream and what I do
> In my weak days are always two,
> Help me, oppressed by things undone,
> O Thou, whose deeds and dreams are one.[2]

Notes

[1]C. S. Lewis, *Mere Christianity* (New York: Macmillan, 1960) 188-89.

[2]John Hunter, as cited in Leslie Tizard, *Preaching: The Art of Communication* (New York: Oxford University Press, 1959) 91-92.

Two Births of Christ

Galatians 4:4-7, 19-20

Vernon Davis

Have you ever been struck by the amazing capacity human beings have to experience the same event in radically different ways? You may sit in church, for example, expecting only a momentary retreat from "the real world" and hoping that in the rehearsal of familiar texts and tunes you will leave feeling better somehow for having come. Another person in the same setting may have come for a quite different reason. With mind fully engaged, that person may be seeking to make sense out of some particular personal problem in light of the theological understanding of the Christian faith. Yet another one sitting beside you may be engaged in a life-and-death struggle of the soul. That worshiper dares to hope that through it all God will become real and that this may become the hinge moment that the future swings open.

Christmas is such an event with many possible meanings. Christmas is a story to be told. It is an affirmation to be believed. It is an experience to be expected. In Christmas we celebrate an event, proclaim a truth, and seek a relationship. Christmas is historical. It is theological and existential. It happened, and it can happen. It is an objective event and a subjective experience. Christmas is then and there; it is here and now. It is both a proclamation and a promise.

Perhaps it seems a bit strange to go to the writings of Paul for the text from which to preach a Christmas sermon. After all, the apostle seldom mentioned the earthly life of Jesus. Paul stated in Galatians 4:4 that Jesus was "born of a woman, born under the law," but these facts give us little to expand our understanding of the event of Jesus' birth itself. Surely, it would be more profitable to mine once again the stories of Luke and Matthew for new or overlooked nuggets in the often-told story of the nativity.

The Christmas possibilities in this difficult Galatians text come from Paul's linking the affirmation of the birth of Christ in Bethlehem with his prayer that Christ be born in us. The gift was given, and the gift keeps on giving. The text keeps us from focusing exclusively on the historical meaning of the birth of Jesus. Of course, we must inevitably begin there, for Christmas is grounded in a stubborn fact of history.

Mary had a baby, and they called his name Jesus. We do not tire of telling and hearing the story. No matter how tarnished the tinsel of our celebration may become or how much those who use the season merely for personal and commercial gain distort its meaning, the story annually demonstrates its amazing resilience. The simple story has refreshing power and remarkable insight into the love of God for us. The variations never do justice to the theme, and the secular substitutes only underscore the power of the simple story. Who has not rejoiced in that thrilling moment when light comes into a child's eyes when he or she hears the words for the first time.

We tell the story again and again. The experienced preacher will approach Christmas wondering how the same story can be told in a fresh way. How can it be that this material will once again speak to contemporary people? Yet it does; for while Christmas is more than a story, it is indeed that. All that has come of Christmas is grounded in an event that really happened, an historically unique occurrence. When all else fails, or better before all else fails, tell the story.

Christmas is also a theological statement, an affirmation of what God was doing in that observable event of history. "In the fullness of time, God sent forth his Son" (Gal 4:4). Such an affirmation comes from living with the story, from recovering with Mary that lost art of pondering and wondering what these things mean. The confident affirmation can ultimately be made only from knowing the end of the story, from reading it only in the light of resurrection and an empty tomb.

Thus, in story and song, in proclamation and pageantry, we seek to declare the inexpressible truth that God has acted in Jesus Christ for us. The birth in Bethlehem has eternal consequences for you and me. The word of Christmas is the truth of how God continues to relate to the world that God created. We declare that the God who is responsible for all that is around us is the God who has come to us in Jesus Christ. We affirm that the God of creation and the God of redemption are the same. With Paul we celebrate: "For God who said, 'Let light shine out of darkness,' made his light shine in our hearts to give us the light of the knowledge of the glory of God in the face of Christ" (2 Cor 4:6).

"God sent forth his Son." In sovereign freedom God acted at the time and in the manner of God's own choosing. The tenacious and tender love of God for the creation is expressed in Bethlehem in a unique way. Christmas forever says that the inexhaustible love of God is unthreatened by human failure and sin.

Martin Luther commented that if he were God and the world had treated him as it had treated God, he would have kicked the thing to bits. We can give thanks that Luther was not God! Instead, in what Phillips Brooks called "the stubborn obstinacy of well-placed affection," God came to us in Jesus. Theologically the mystery is best stated in the words of John: "The word became flesh and made his dwelling among us. We have seen his glory, the glory of the One and Only, who came from the Father, full of grace and truth" (John 1:14).

The phrase "born of a woman, born under the law" does more than attest the historical event of Jesus' birth. For Paul the reality of Jesus' humanity was vitally important theologically. One who was not like us could not redeem us. One who did not share our humanity could not become our savior.

Paul's letters affirm the genuineness of Jesus' humanity. Jesus did not pass through history as one who only seemed to be human.

He shared the limitations of humanity, yet he was without sin. Christmas is a time to proclaim the truth of the humanity of the divine Son of God.

I am convinced, however, that the part of the text that we most need today is neither the reminder of the ancient story nor the reaffirmation of its theological truth. Paul wrote to Christians who knew the story well and believed that Jesus was the Son of God. Their attitudes and actions, however, revealed how little they really understood and experienced him. The Galatians had difficulty living freely in grace. They gave little evidence that they had been fully informed or empowered by the Son.

In an expression of deep compassion, Paul addressed the Galatians as "My dear children, for whom I am again in the pains of childbirth until Christ is formed in you" (Gal 4:19). The heart of Paul consistently went out to those who had access to God's revelation but had not fully experienced it. He was troubled by those who lived as if the birth of Christ had not happened. For them he prayed for an experience that could be compared to a birth of Christ in them.

The image created by Paul's words is both powerful and confusing. He likened himself to a childbearing mother who is in travail. He expressed the intense pain he was enduring in order that those who read his words would experience the spiritual birth of Christ within them. His singular desire was that they would be formed in their inner persons into likeness of Jesus Christ. The imagery is difficult because at times it seems that it is Paul who was enduring the labor and the people who were expected to bring forth the child. Nevertheless, it conveys the astounding truth that the miracle of the incarnation, which happened uniquely in Jesus' birth in Bethlehem, can also happen in us. It is both possible and necessary for there to be two births of Christ, one forever fixed as an indisputable fact of history and the other happening again and again in the hearts of believers in every age.

The poet Angelus Silesius, whose real name was John Scheffler, said: "Were Christ born in Bethlehem a thousand times and not in you, you would be eternally lost." The birth of Jesus in Bethlehem was a pivotal event in human history, and many things are different in our culture because of it. Human beings, however, do not experience the meaning of this event for themselves by some process of cultural osmosis. Through our response of faith in him, Jesus Christ must be born in us.

Emil Brunner said:

> There must really take place in us something corresponding to what once happened in Bethlehem: a birth through the Holy Ghost. . . . Through the gospel of Jesus Christ and the faith of the believer, a new man must come into being, a man in Christ, and this new life is not intended to be merely inward, but to manifest itself outwardly and bring forth its appropriate fruits.[1]

This possibility is the real promise in the celebration of Christmas. Until Christ is formed in us, the story of Jesus' birth can seem to be only about something long ago and far away, dwelling within the realm of fantasy and the world of children. If Christ can be born in us, everything is changed. The Word becomes flesh again and again, dwelling within and among human beings in desperate need of hope. Then the story becomes believable in every time and place.

In his poem, "Kitty Hawk," Robert Frost said:

> But God's own descent
> Into flesh was meant
> As a demonstration
> That the supreme merit
> Lay in risking spirit
>   in substantiation.
>
>   . . . .
> Spirit enters flesh
> And for all it's worth
> Charges in to earth
> In birth after birth
> Ever fresh, ever fresh.[2]

The birth we need today involves both pain and process. We would be far more receptive to the challenge if it did not. If somehow what was being asked of us were only the telling of a story and affirming of a truth, we would be more comfortable. If only it were a matter of memorizing scripture, and learning the doctrine, and preaching the sermon, but having the image of Christ formed in us requires much more. Our hearts must become stable; our lives must be open to the reception of God's gift that changes everything within us.

We are reluctant to open ourselves in that way to anyone. We entertain the possibility only because closing out the Christ has resulted in ache and emptiness that no remedy is able to reach. We cannot stand the contradiction of telling the story of Jesus and reciting the doctrine about him while at the same time failing to experience his living reality in our inner lives. We struggle to find the words to express our deep need and discover them in the prayer penned long ago by Phillips Brooks:

> O holy child of Bethlehem!
> Descend to us, we pray;
> Cast out our sin, and enter in,
> Be born in us today!
> We hear the Christmas angels
> The great glad tidings tell;
> O come to us, abide with us,
> Our Lord Immanuel![3]

Notes

[1]*The Great Invitation* (Philadelphia: Westminster, 1955) 147.

[2]*The Poetry of Robert Frost* (New York: Holt, Rinehart and Winston, 1979) 435–36.

[3]"O Little Town of Bethlehem," *The Baptist Hymnal* (Nashville: Convention Press, 1991) 86.

Playing with the Promise

Galatians 4:21-31

Scott Nash

The closing stanza of one of Rabindranath Tagore's Nobel prize-winning poems reads:

> On the seashore of endless worlds
> children meet.
> Tempest roams in the pathless sky,
> Ships get wrecked in the trackless water,
> Death is abroad and children play.
> On the seashore of endless worlds
> is the great meeting of children.[1]

The stanza is a poignant ending to a poem that depicts human beings as children content to play on the edge of the depths of life, naively oblivious to both the terrors and treasures that lie in the great deep and in the great beyond. The children build their sand castles, collect their shells, and set sail their little leaf-woven boats. The sea playfully frolics with the children and smiles at them with its long, narrow sandy lips.

This poem is one of the best presentations I know of the contrast between the pleasures and perils of childhood, or of approaching life from the perspective of childhood, which among many other possible images could be characterized as a life of "play." When we think of children or of our own childhoods, the image that often comes to mind is that of play. Childhood is a time for play, or at least we generally believe that it should be.

For many children in this world today, life is filled with everything but play. It is filled with the horrors of hunger, violence, abuse, and the struggle for survival. Even as we remind ourselves of the harsh realities that numerous children have to suffer, however, we view their pain as abnormal. They should not have to endure such affliction. They should be granted the rights of childhood, the rights of enjoying life, the freedom to play as children. Childhood is a time for play, not a time for imposing the cold responsibilities and irresponsibilities of adult life upon those least prepared to handle them. Healthy advancement toward adulthood requires a time for play, a time for being children.

And for healthy adults, time should also be allowed for play—time for release from the pressures and responsibilities of life. "All work and no play makes Jack a dull boy," I am reminded by a childhood proverb. Eternal seriousness can rob us of the enjoyment of life's many blessings. We need children around us to remind us of these blessings, and sometimes, for a little while, we need to become children ourselves again to experience these blessings.

One problem for adults, of course, is that playtime can become an obsession. The pursuit of pleasure can override our sense of responsibility. We can seek personal enjoyment to the detriment of ourselves and others when "playing" with life becomes our total approach to living. Perhaps our Puritan forebears realized this when they advocated total sobriety and seriousness in living. Perhaps the rigidity they espoused was their reaction to what they perceived to be the perilous side of allowing childish ways to linger too long into adulthood. The dangers of approaching life irresponsibly are painfully apparent in the toil of lives wasted to indulgence in addictive substances and to intoxication with "having a good time." The peril of childish play is obvious; the solution of imposing rigidity, of eliminating or at least controlling the playful spirit, can become attractive.

Perhaps Paul's opponents in Galatia believed that Paul's brand of Christianity was childishly irresponsible. Perhaps they saw the Gentile converts who had responded to his preaching of the gospel as grown-up children who needed to be led, or forced, into a more adult, responsible understanding of the faith. After all, those Gentiles had not had the same benefit of a strong, moral upbringing that the Jewish Christians had to help them control their excesses. The gospel of freedom in Christ that Paul espoused was just one more invitation to total freedom of the human spirit, and, as all good Jews and Jewish Christians of the time knew, the Gentiles were already "loose" enough in their indulgences. They needed adult guidance. They needed to know where the limits were, and the best set of limits available to them was the code of conduct enshrined in the Mosaic tradition. If they could only be persuaded to follow that tradition, then they could be rescued from their infantile immorality and really "saved."

Paul's reaction to the efforts of his opponents was intense—some of his opponents might have even called it predictably childish. He lashed out at those advocating the Law as the remedy for Gentile irresponsibility and at those Gentile Christians who had been persuaded to accept it with even more sharpness than was typical for the feisty apostle. He accused his opponents of "playing" with the genuine faith of the Galatians and, even more seriously, of "playing" loosely with the gospel itself. What the opponents were actually doing, according to Paul, was robbing the Galatians of their childhood. They were stealing their status as children of God. They were trying to convert them from being children of the promise to being children of slavery, and slavery, Paul reminded them, had little in common with real childhood at all. He didn't want anyone playing around with his children's promise.

Whenever someone insists that our status as children of God through faith in Jesus Christ must be "corrected" by certain humanly-conceived rules, then we need to question whether or not they are playing around with our promise, too. Especially when they insist that their way of seeing and doing is THE way God sees it, we need to raise questions, because "playing" God is one of the most "childish" behaviors that adults ever commit. When we are told that there is only one way of understanding what the Bible says or what the Bible is, we need to be cautious. When we are told that there is only one way of understanding what a Christian is, we need to be concerned. When we are told who can and cannot serve God in certain ways, we need to be especially alarmed because there is something in the voice of those who make such claims that is alien to the voice of Jesus himself. When we hear such orders to do this and that from those who claim the authority of God, we may even be prompted to respond with the same intensity that moved Paul to his strongly-worded argument in Galatians. We may even find ourselves echoing his sharp wish that they "cut it out" (Gal 5:12).

Paul's response to the activity of his opponents, however well-intentioned they may have been, was unambiguously belligerent. Too much was at stake to be gentle. Yet, his argument for his understanding of the gospel was not irrational. He presented a carefully constructed defense, following an effective rhetorical scheme the Roman legal experts of his day would have appreciated (which says something about the breadth of Paul's Jewish seminary education!). He stated his view, recalled how and why he had come to this position, and then mustered to his side a series of "proofs." He reasoned sensibly and presented evidence from Scripture to support his views.

For his final "proof," however, Paul engaged in a very "playful" interpretation of Scripture (Gal 4:21-31). He reminded the Galatians of the story in Genesis about Hagar and Sarah (Gen 16 and 21). Abraham had been given a son by each of these two women. They could read this story for themselves. What they could not read for themselves was Paul's new interpretation. "This story is an *allegory*," Paul said. It's a story with a hidden meaning, Paul was saying, and I'll tell you what the hidden meaning is.

Now Paul wasn't alone in reading his Bible this way. The Greeks had been reinterpreting their old stories of gods and goddesses this way for a long time. The Jews had also sometimes used the method to find new meanings in old texts. It became a popular way of understanding the Bible later on in the church; in fact, the allegorical approach even became the most commonly accepted way to read Scripture, up until the time of the Reformation. The concern for historical and linguistic faithfulness to the original text that came out of the Reformation has largely led to the discrediting of such allegorical treatments of Scripture today, but for a large part of the church's history such a "playful" reading of Scripture has been seen as a legitimate way to hear the word of God. The problem with such an approach, of course, is that the only "control" for the results obtained is the personal limitation of the creativity and imagination of the interpreter.

Paul was perhaps at his creative best when he retold this story of Hagar and Sarah. "The two women are two covenants," he said (Gal 4:24). "One, Hagar, stands for Mount Sinai"—the place whence the Law came. "Hagar is a mountain in Arabia," he reminded them (calling also to their minds that Paul had spent time in Arabia and presumably knew about such things; Gal 1:17), "but Hagar is also that mountain in Palestine called Jerusalem"—the place whence his Law-toting opponents had come (Gal 4:25). "The child of that woman is a child born of the flesh and born into slavery." "But the other woman/covenant," Paul asserted, "is the heavenly Jerusalem not bound by the Law, and her child is the free child of the promise born by the Spirit."

Telling the story this way allowed Paul to do what all good storytellers do—draw their listeners right into the story. "Now which woman is your mother?" was the implied question for the Galatians. "Right," Paul said, articulating their own answer, "you, my friends, are the children of the promise, like Isaac" (Gal 4:28). "And what is more," Paul's retelling of the story pointed out, "the Galatians were experiencing at the hands of his opponents the same kind of 'persecution' that Isaac encountered from Ishmael, the child of the flesh" (Gal 4:29).

Now here Paul was especially playful with the text. Genesis 21 doesn't say that Ishmael "persecuted" Isaac. In fact, Genesis 21:9 says that Sarah saw Ishmael "playing" with Isaac. But already by Paul's time Jewish tradition had elevated Ishmael's actions to that of "ridiculing" and "picking on" Isaac, and the history of relations between Jews and "Ishmaelites" (Arabs) had even then often been one of animosity. The idea of the child of the promise being persecuted by the child of the flesh was already entrenched in the Jewish psyche.

What Paul did was reverse the identities of the children and claim that those who assumed they were the children of the promise—the Jews and Jewish Christians—were actually the children of Hagar and were persecuting the true children of Sarah—the Gentile Christians who were not bound by the Law. His opponents were guilty of siding with Ishmael and "playing with" or "picking on" the actual children of the promise. Their actions endangered their own claim to childhood because they stood dangerously close to experiencing the harsh sentence pronounced upon Hagar and her slave-child: "Drive out the slave and her child; for the child of the slave will not share the inheritance with the child of the free woman" (Gal 4:30; Gen 21:10).

One problem the religious hall monitors have is that they deprive themselves of grace when they withhold it from those they seek to bring under their own regulatory systems. Even when their motivations are sincere and they are trying to do their best to "save people from a sinner's hell," they risk making their new convert "twice as much a child of hell" as they themselves already are (Matt 23:15). Their call is to share the misery of their sad company, "cut off" from the enjoyment of the promise of God's unconditional grace through faith in Jesus Christ.

For Paul, the price his opponents exacted for bringing the possible excesses of freedom under control was too high. Surely, the Galatians, and other new converts, needed guidance on how to enjoy their status as children of the promise, children of God—Paul never questioned the need for guidance, as his numerous ethical

injunctions in his letters testify. But the answer was not to eliminate the "childly" nature of their childhood. It was not to thrust
them into a world where rigidity, conformity, and obeisance to
rules and rulers shaped their lives into such narrow confines.

The answer to the dilemma of childhood lay in the very grace
that had birthed them. It lay in standing fast in the freedom granted
to them by God through Christ (Gal 5:1). It lay in bringing their
living under the only "rule" large enough to embrace the promise:
"You shall love your neighbor as yourself" (Gal 5:14). By love
they had been born anew; by love they would live as free children.

The way advocated by Paul is a dangerous way; one could even
call it reckless, maybe even irresponsible. It holds no guarantees,
save that the one who set us on this way holds our lives and will
not let us go. It cannot ensure "correct" behavior. In fact, this way
of freedom and faith carries the probability that the children who
travel its paths will stumble and fall. Such is the price of learning
to walk, a price far less costly than never walking at all.

The children who set out on this way of the promise will often,
too often for comfort, find themselves without a specific rule to
guide their steps. They will often stand on the edge of the great
mystery wondering what to do. They do not have all the answers.
They are children. They should play. They should play "with the
promise." They should live and love, not in fear of taking the
wrong step but in the light of the promise that the God who loved
them into life loves them still and always will, naughty or nice.

On that great seashore of endless worlds, where unfathomable
love lurks in the depths and waves its graceful smiles to the faithful on the beach, is the great meeting of children.

Note

[1]From *Gitanjali*, no. 60.

The Great
Grace Adventure

Galatians 5:1-6

Ronda Stewart-Wilcox

The world is an unsafe place. We are constantly reminded of that. We see it on the morning news. We read it in the daily paper. Even commercials remind us of our fears by playing on them, encouraging us to buy whatever security measure they are trying to sell. Sometimes politicians play on our fears to get votes. And occasionally, things happen to us to bring home how fragile our security is.

Recently, my husband, Rodney, was in a pretty good car accident. It was *good* in the sense that if Rodney's aim had been to wreck our car totally, he would have been very successful. I was on the scene not long after it had happened. My heart was almost in my throat as I drove up to the place where it had occurred. I expected to see a couple of cars with minor dents, but instead I saw our car turned at a totally improbable angle with half a dozen uniformed people busy around it. The fire truck was there, which made me fear the possibility of fire. I think there were at least two police vehicles, but I am not sure. What I definitely saw in that chaos was our car. Rodney was not standing anywhere in the crowd. Sure enough, as I approached the car, I saw him in the driver's seat hanging on to the steering wheel while paramedics checked his pulse and blood pressure and secured his neck and back. My heart leaped into my throat! Just as quickly I realized that he was mostly fine, but in those few seconds of uncertainty I feared the worst. I realized that I could have lost more than a new car that day. And that realization shook me to the bones.

Rodney is safe, now. His injuries were very minor. The car was totalled, but we already have a new and improved car to replace it. The whole affair hasn't even really cost us that much money. But for a moment in our lives, time stopped as we held our breath and waited to know—were we safe or lost?

Rodney has been nervous about driving since then, particularly in the morning hours when his accident occurred. It took him awhile to start driving again at all. He was anxious for a bit about even riding as a passenger in a car. (Of course, he's never been *really* comfortable with my driving anyway.)

Rodney could have stopped driving altogether. What happened was pretty scary stuff. Some drivers on the road do some pretty stupid things that we don't have any control over. How can we be *sure* that something like this will never happen again?

One way to be sure is never to drive again. If Rodney never drives again, then he won't have another accident in a car. But, then, I guess I had better not drive anymore either. And we won't be able to ride in anyone else's car—not if we want to be *really* sure of our safety from car accidents. I live just across the street from the church where I work. Oh, but I have to cross the street. If I really want to avoid any accidents with a car, I had better not cross the street. We can never be sure that some driver won't lose control and hit me as I am walking to work. I guess we'll just have to stay in our house and never go anywhere.

Yeah, right! I never want to be a prisoner in my own home. I like the freedom of being able to walk to work. I like the freedom of being able to buy my own groceries and going to meetings in town. I like driving across country to visit family and friends.

We can't be sure we will never have another car accident. Gosh. That has been such a hard lesson for me to learn. We can't be sure about much of anything. As a child, I was very shy and very afraid that people wouldn't like me. I remember asking my mother, "How can I be sure that they will like me?" The answer is we can't be sure. Some people will like us, some won't. We may go a very long time without an accident, but one day we or someone we love may be in one. We may never be robbed. We may never get seriously ill. The choices we make may be the right ones or at least the best ones; they may not. We simply cannot guarantee that everything we do will always be the best thing for our lives.

The Galatians seem to have been trying to find that kind of guarantee. The Galatians were Greeks, not Jews. Paul had shared with them Christ's good news, and they had made the best choice of their lives—they had believed.

As Greeks, they had not participated in the Jewish practice of circumcising their infant sons. Naturally. It was not expected of them. But circumcision was expected for a Jewish male and for male converts to Judaism. Circumcision was part of the covenant between God and Abraham and, thus, part of the continuing covenant between God and his people. It was a mark of citizenship in the nation of Israel. To be a Jew was to be circumcised. This was very important for a man and his family. It was part of the Law. The Christian Jews still practiced much of the Law, including circumcision. Why not? Christ did say that he had come to fulfill the Law, not to abolish it.

But the Christian Galatians were not Jews. Should they be expected to follow the Jewish law now that they were Christians? That is what we say to immigrants and new citizens of our nation. "You are in America now. You left behind one culture and one set of laws. Now you need to submit to our culture and our set of laws." Visitors and immigrants have to promise to abide by our laws. New citizens take an oath to uphold and defend our laws. It only makes sense. We need rules to keep order. People are just exchanging one set of rules for another—they hope, better—set of rules.

I am sure that this is what some people were telling the Galatian Christians. Once you were Gentile, but now you believe in God and so you must obey God's laws. It is such a reasonable argument, I almost believe it myself.

But Paul did not fall for that kind of faulty logic. And it was faulty. He tells us, "For freedom Christ has set us free" (5:1). Christ set us free from our sins, but not to enslave us. He does not want us to exchange one slavery for another.

When some people stop smoking, they start eating. Then they have to learn to stop eating too much. Some people learn the joy and freedom of a healthy body made possible by exercise, and then they become obsessive about exercising so that it controls their life. Some people, upon being set free from school at graduation, become slaves to their work. The sexual revolution of the 1960s set many people free from their inhibitions only to enslave them to the consequences of their unrestrained sexual appetites.

Very often we exchange one set of rules for another. We like rules. They give structure to our lives. They help define what is meaningful and important. They provide a measure of security. They can help answer questions in times of uncertainty. We don't have to think so hard, because some things have already been decided for us. We don't have to take so many risks. I know I frequently am looking for what is the "right" thing to do.

Paul is telling us that Christ set us free to be free. I am not sure, however, that we really like that kind of freedom. I taught high school for awhile. My students often complained that I graded too hard or too easy, that I gave too few or too many assignments. But when I gave them a choice of assignments, they couldn't think of anything to do. They would come to me to ask "What should I do?" Some of them got very angry at me for *not* telling them what to do. When I gave them the opportunity to grade their own papers, they refused to do it. They were uncomfortable with the freedom they had, and they wanted me to take control again.

How scary freedom really is! Do you remember being on your own for the first time? Did you call home a lot for all kinds of advice? Maybe you didn't call home, but did you want to? How do I know my choices are the right ones? How do I know which to choose? Gotta think! Gotta listen! Gotta learn! It's frustrating. It's challenging. I've got to think for myself. Even now, there are times when I want someone else to make the decisions for me. Some of those decisions are really just too scary to deal with.

But what happens when we exchange one set of rules for another? Paul told the Galatians that if they submitted to the circumcision of Jewish law, they would be cutting themselves off from Christ. I think Paul uses the term "cut" quite deliberately to drive home the point that the cutting they propose to endure will cut off more than they expect. It will cut them off from the grace Christ has offered to them.

Grace is the key for Paul and for us. The Law demands that we keep every atomic-sized bit of it. But we can't. One stray, improper thought condemns us. One missed opportunity to do a good deed, condemns us. One angry word, one small mistake, one tiny error, condemns us. We cannot keep all of the Law. We can try, but the Law doesn't recognize try. My husband did not intend to have a car accident. In fact, he tried not to, but he had one anyway. How many times have you been as careful as can be, and still you goofed up? How many times have you acted on good intentions only to accomplish the opposite goal? We are not *able* to keep the Law.

The grace of Christ recognizes that we continually miss the mark. The grace of Christ knows that even the most diligent, well-intentioned of us makes mistakes. The grace of Christ says, "You are forgiven for making mistakes and missing the mark." The grace of Christ sets us free from keeping a Law that we are not able to keep. And that is why Paul is so upset with the Galatians.

Do you know what an adventure is? Certain movies and stories come to mind when I think of "adventure": "Raiders of the Lost Ark"; Perceval searching for the Holy Grail; a good old John Wayne western; "City Slickers." An adventure is exciting, thrilling, even if we are only watching it on the screen. It's suspenseful; we don't know what is going to happen next. Will Indiana Jones be able to rescue the Lost Ark from the Nazis and stay alive? Will Percival ever find the Holy Grail? Will John Wayne live or die?

Will Billy Crystal survive his vacation in one piece? There is risk involved in adventure. I guess that is what makes it so exciting!

The dictionary definition of "adventure" is "a bold undertaking, in which hazards are to be met and the issue hangs upon unforeseen events; a daring feat." Paul was involved in the greatest adventure ever, and he wanted the Galatians to be his sidekicks and go along with him.

An adventure has many risks and the promise of great reward. Indiana Jones faced many risks. He faced death and bodily harm many times. Still he pursued the prize: to recover the lost Ark of the Covenant, a prize so valuable that he had to compete with German Nazis for its possession.

The adventure of Christ's grace has many risks and the promise of great reward. Paul was imprisoned. He survived stoning and shipwreck. His body bore the scars of the persecution he encountered. Still he pursued the prize, the prize he described in his letter to the Philippians as "the heavenly call of God in Christ Jesus." (Phil 3:14) He pursued the prize Christ offers: grace and freedom from missing the mark.

The Galatians wanted the prize; there is no doubt about that. I think that is why Paul was so upset. He saw that the Galatians were doing all they could to gain the prize. It's just that they were doing the wrong things. In trying to gain the prize, they were making the mistake of cutting themselves off from it. They were trying to hedge their bet, but in so doing they were going to lose it. By submitting to circumcision, they were submitting to the entire Law. They were turning to the Law for their salvation, but the Law is not forgiving. One mistake and you are lost. They were looking for a sure thing—and giving up everything they had.

Before we start feeling very righteous, we need to remember that we do the very same thing. Of course we don't submit ourselves to the Jewish Law as the Galatians were doing, but we, too, look for security and surety. Though we love to read about adventure and watch adventure movies, we don't really like to be in the middle of one. It *is* hazardous and risky and scary. We want the safest, surest route to reach our goal.

Today we look for rules and laws, just as the Galatians did. In freedom we are not always sure that we are traveling the right road. How often have you turned to the Bible hoping for an answer to a very specific question, "What should I do about . . . ?" How often have you found a specific answer for that specific question?

Today people turn to psychics for "all the answers." After all, Mickie Dane "knows." People look for gurus. We look for people to tell us the answers to life's difficult questions. But when we let other people make our decisions for us, we turn our lives over to them. We no longer are free to make our decisions for ourselves. We find ourselves abiding by other people's values and expectations. We find ourselves slaves to other people's view of the way life should be. We take jobs we don't really want. We marry people we don't really love. We attend schools we don't want to go to.

I joined a sorority in college, not because I wanted to, but because I *thought* my mother wanted me to. Consequently, I was not very happy, simply because it hadn't really been my choice. I wasn't free to enjoy it. What have you done because you allowed someone else to choose *for* you?

Life's questions *are* difficult! How much easier it would be if there were pre-set answers to the dilemmas and crises we face! Then we only would have to look in the back of the textbook at the answer page, just like we used to do in math.

Do you remember looking up the answers to your math problems in the back of the book? Usually, though, the book only listed the answers to all the odd questions or to all the even questions, but not for all the questions. Of course, the back of the book didn't tell us the steps to take between the statement of the problem and the answer. My brother could figure out the steps between if he had the stated problem and the answer. He would look in the back for the final answer, and then he knew what the steps in between should be to reach that answer.

But we don't have the final answer to all our problems. We have to figure out the answer and the steps in between all by ourselves. Or do we?

I think Paul is saying to the Galatians and to us that we do have the final answer: Christ's gift of grace and freedom to us. But we have to be the ones to choose. I have to choose. You have to choose. No one else can choose it for us. The Judaizers can't choose for the Galatians. We can't allow our parents' desires, our spouse's wishes, our friends' good intentions, our teachers, our pastors to decide for us. *We* must be the ones to choose.

We can't let other things be the substitute for the Answer. The Galatians, though they were confused and unaware of this, were substituting the Law for the Answer. We, too, must not make substitutions: a set of rules to follow, a set of acts performed and recognized, a list of facts stated. The Answer is to join in the adventure of accepting the grace Christ offers us. The adventure is remaining free from the temptation to submit to anyone or anything other than Christ. The adventure is trusting Christ, having faith in Christ.

A word of caution: trusting, believing, having faith are not acts of the mind. We often separate our minds, spirits, hearts, and bodies so that what happens in one seems to have no effect or connection to any of the others. We can say we believe the earth is round without ever having to act as if the earth is actually round. We talk about how our heart says one thing and our mind says another. We talk about the need to quit smoking or lose weight or start exercising, but our bodies rarely see the benefit because we don't act on the very knowledge we say we believe.

When Paul talks about faith, he does not limit faith to an act of the mind. Faith is an act of the entire person: mind, body, soul, heart. Christ tells to love God with all our heart and soul and mind and strength. Loving God is an act of the entire person. When we have faith, we live faith. What our mind believes is acted on by our bodies and lives in our hearts and souls. We become a complete person of faith, so that what we believe is how we live, even to the tiniest thought or action.

Paul tells the Galatians and us that "the only thing that counts is faith [in Christ] working through love." Faith in the Law does not count. Faith in other people does not count. Faith in the textbook answer does not count. The only thing that will lead us to the prize in this great grace adventure is the faith that lives in our entire person, in all aspects of our lives. If we give even one part of our life over to someone or something else, then we are cut off from the prize Christ offers: the freedom to be faithful followers of Christ.

Christian Freedom and Positive Morality

Galatians 5:13–6:10

W. Clyde Tilley

Galatians, along with Romans and Ephesians, is so structured as to accentuate the connection between doctrine and ethics. An extended section on Christian theology (what Christians should believe) introduces the epistle, and a subsequent section on Christian ethics (how Christians should behave) follows and concludes it. The lifestyle of the Christian grows out of the rich soil of Christian theology. In the Christian faith, these two components have frequently and aptly been called the divine indicative—what God has done on our behalf—and the divine imperative—what God requires of us.

In Galatians, this great divide is between chapters four and five. After defending his apostleship (chapters 1–2), which the Judaizers had attacked, Paul proceeded to present the doctrine of Christian freedom (chapters 3–4). Then in the last two chapters he came to speak of the Christian life that is to be lived out in the context of freedom.

It was essential that Paul not conclude his letter before doing this. The doctrine of Christian freedom is especially vulnerable to misinterpretation. It is subject to two perils that Paul's extended warning takes into account. The first peril is the most obvious one and has occasioned the letter, that of legalism, the repudiation of Christian freedom, which Judaizers advocated. Thus Paul addressed this peril in his first and shortest section on the life of Christian freedom (5:1-12), a peril that agitated Paul from the letter's start.

The second peril is that of lawlessness or libertinism. This peril differs from the first in that while the first is a clear-cut alternative, this one is a perversion of freedom and has a superfical resemblance to it. Having heard the gospel of freedom from the law of Moses, it would be easy for well-meaning believers to surmise that the Christian life is one of lawlessness. It would also be easy, and likely had occurred in the case of the Galatians, for the enemies of this gospel to caricature it as such. But Paul could not let silence give tacit consent to this misunderstanding and so proceeded to disavow any such interpretation in the passage before us (5:13–6:10).

The unity of this passage can be defended in the light of Paul's overriding concern throughout that Christian morality does have a positive content. He wanted both to show what this positive content is and how it is dynamically operative in the life of the Christian believer. Although we have freedom from Moses' law in the light of our justification by faith in Christ, the readers needed to be reminded that there is still (1) a law of love (5:13-15), (2) a life of the Spirit (5:16-26), (3) a law of maturity (6:1-6), and (4) a law of the harvest (6:7-10).

The Law of Love (5:13–15)

The opening line brings together the notion of the Christian's call, a notion Paul never tired of stressing, and that of freedom, the heartbeat of his letter. Earlier he had spoken of God as one who had "called you in the grace of Christ" (1:6).[1] Now they "were called to freedom," a necessary sequel to divine grace. The Christian's call is central to their comprising a church, "the called out ones." Just as Paul had earlier characterized their call as one "in grace," he here characterized it as one "to (or for) freedom."

Verse 13 both serves to summarize Paul's message up until now and to launch a new warning. He urged that they not "use [their] freedom as an opportunity for self-indulgence [literally, flesh]." In championing freedom over the law and from the law, Paul could not leave the floodgate of freedom open to the tide of lawlessness that would plague every Christian generation (Cf. Rom. 6:1-2). How tragic if, in seeking to avoid the Scylla of legalism, they should find themselves shipwrecked on the Carybdis of lawlessness!

The word translated "opportunity" literally suggests the notion of "a starting point" or "a launching pad." Does the dismantling of the law, which had earlier endeavored to restrain the flesh, simply mean the cleaning off of a place to be used as a launching pad from which the flesh may be sent on its way without restraint? Paul's answer is a strong denial and prohibition.

The reason such might suggest itself to the uninitiated hearer is that the structure and range of authentic freedom is rarely fully appreciated. Freedom has both negative and positive counterparts; it involves a freedom *from* and a freedom *to*.[2] To see the Christian's freedom as only a freedom from the law is an inadequate grasp. It is also a freedom to, with a positive content. In contrast to using freedom as a launching pad for fleshly indulgence, we must "through love become slaves to one another." We are not only free *from* the law; we are free *to* serve each other.

Here we encounter a paradox of the starkest sort. Freedom in Christ means a new slavery. The notion of "servant" is too anemic; Paul's choice of a word bids us see our new role as that of a "slave." Far from being freed to do anything we want to, we are freed to be at each other's disposal.

What then is the superiority of the new slavery over the old? It is simply this: in the new slavery it is "through love" that we serve. The work of love, as far as the most objectionable features of work are concerned, is no work at all. It was the consideration of love that prompted John to say, "We obey his commandments, and his commandments are not burdensome" (1 John 5:3). One is reminded of Jacob's work for his beloved Rachael of whom it is said that "seven years . . . seemed to him but a few days because of the love that he had for her" (Gen 29: 20). There is no bondage in doing what one delights to do, even if it fulfills a requirement.

The prophets envisioned the supercession of the old covenant with its law by a new covenant. Jeremiah spoke for God: "I will put my law within them, and I will write it on their hearts" (Jer 31:33). This labor of love not only ceases to be burdensome; only when it becomes a labor of love does it also become fully moral. In this context, the chasm between doing what I want to do and doing what God bids me do loses much of its intimidation.

But it is possible to oversentimentalize this labor of love. It is still a law to be obeyed (v. 14) even when the love that motivates us is lacking in its perfection. The law of love is perfect even when our love is not. Paul must have been familiar with the way our Lord summed up the law in the two great commandments (Matt 22:33-40). He used the law of neighbor-love in the same way here (Cf. 6:2) as did John (1 John 2: 7-11), who called it a new commandment, and James (2:8), who called it the royal law. Paul presented it as the all-inclusive and self-sufficient law, as did our Lord along with love for God (Matt 22:40). The law itself is from the Old Testament (Lev 19:18) but towers like a mountain peak over the rest (or we may say that it is a range that includes all the rest). It may not be too ambitious to say for this law that had we only understood it and obeyed it maturely, we would need no guidance from any other.

In addition to the mission of love that this commandment alerts us to, the measure of love is also given. They were not only to love their neighbors; they were to love them as themselves. It accepts and reinforces a proper love for ourselves rather than discouraging it. To love our neighbor as ourselves is not only difficult to do but, because of the subjective nature of this love, it is also difficult to be sure when we are doing so. Linus Pauling once said, "Do unto others twenty per cent better than they do unto you and thus eliminate the subjective element."[3]

Three observations need to be made with regard to verse 15.

(1) This is in some sense the antithesis and negative counterpart of love. So exalted is the commandment of love that it is extremely difficult to capture its negative counterpart in a prohibitive law, but

this was Paul's unimpressive attempt. Love certainly precludes biting and devouring one another and much else that falls between the wide cracks.

(2) Paul's appeal to the command of love was never on the grounds of prudence alone. But it is a prudent commandment, and Paul did not hesitate to call attention to it. Those who behave in unloving ways are bound to leave themselves open to the same kinds of affronts—in this case, biting and devouring.

(3) Paul's injunction against biting and devouring surely reflected the state of affairs that had come about as a result of the work of Judaizers. Not only did they threaten the truth of the gospel by their teaching, but they also undermined the fellowship of the church by their intrusion.

The Life of the Spirit (5:16–26)

The early verses of this passage where Paul was describing the moral struggle in the human life is reminiscent of Romans 7. However, this difference must be observed. There he described the struggle in the unregenerate heart, leading him to conclude: "I can will what is right but I cannot do it. For I do not do the good I want, but the evil I do not want is what I do" (Rom 7: 18-19).

Here, on the other hand, Paul described the moral struggle in the life of the redeemed individual. He appropriated the word "Spirit" to the Holy Spirit in verse 16 and never relinquishes its usage to the human spirit throughout the passage. Paul's major concern, as in the previous paragraph, was that Christian freedom not deteriorate or be perverted into a libertine lifestyle. There he had summoned the virtue of love to safeguard against it. Here he asserted the life of the Spirit to whom he would later trace love as a part of the Spirit's fruit (v. 22).

The only imperative statement in this passage is the opening one: "Live (or walk about) by the Spirit." To translate the rest of the verse as "do not gratify the desires of the flesh" (as in NRSV) is to ignore the grammar and perhaps to distort the meaning. It is not as though a second command is being laid alongside the first. It is the claim that by walking by the Spirit, the gratification of fleshly desires will be precluded. The question under consideration is how can we avoid lawlessness if the law of Moses is no longer operative. Paul's answer was the life of the Spirit. Just as the command of love can prevent lawlessness when viewed from one perspective, the life of the Spirit can do so when viewed from another.

Paul then depicted the antithesis between the flesh with its desires and the Spirit with the Spirit's desires (v. 17). This antithesis is heightened by the two parallel statements in this verse as well as by the summary statement that "these are opposed to each other." Just as we observed that "Spirit" in this passage always refers to the Holy Spirit, we need also to clarify the sense in which "flesh" is being used. The flesh is more than the body, the sensuality of nerve endings and the cravings they can incite in the brain. It rather indicates the whole panorama of that which the lower human nature controls when the Spirit is not permitted to do so. This is perfectly clear from the works of the flesh later to be listed (vv. 19-21).

When Paul cited this opposition between flesh and Spirit as being "to prevent you from doing what you want," he probably intended to speak of the purpose of this opposition and not just its result. And if this is purposive, it will speak of the purpose of the Spirit in preventing what the flesh wants rather than the purpose of the flesh in preventing what the Spirit wants. In fact, Paul's overriding concern was to answer the objection that if there is no law, what is there "to prevent you from doing what you want [i. e., anything you please]"? His answer was the Spirit of God when one walks in that Spirit.

Living or walking by the Spirit harbors two subsidiary notions. One is that of power and one is that of guidance. To live by the Spirit is to be sustained by the Spirit's power and to be led by the Spirit's guidance. Paul later divided these notions (v. 25), but here we have the notion of the Spirit's guidance accentuated (v. 18). A basic assumption of Judaism was that the function of the law was to give moral guidance unto salvation. The Judaizers continued to sound that theme. But Paul wanted to disavow any truth in that claim. Being led by the Spirit leaves no room for our subjection to the law. Just as the Spirit and the flesh are mutually exclusive in their guidance, so are the Spirit and the law mutually exclusive in the guidance they offer. The adequacy of the Spirit to keep us from doing "anything we please" is set in contrast to the earlier inadequacy of the law for doing the same thing.

The flesh and the Spirit, desiring differently (v. 17), produce differently as well. The fifteen fleshly works that Paul enumerated are incomplete as a list and sometimes lacking in specificity. The incompleteness is seen by the addition of the phrase: "and things like this" (v. 21). These are referred to as non-specific because of the interpreters' sometime inability to define the works specifically and a tendency of the list at times to overlap or leave gaps. Perhaps the clearest thing to be done in so little space is to organize these works into four groupings and to characterize the groupings.

The first three obviously belong together: fornication, impurity, and licentiousness (v. 19). As noted above, the flesh is more than sensuality. But it does include that. These are the most direct ways the flesh manifests itself when dominant (1 Cor 6:18). *Fornication* denotes pre-marital sex in our culture but cannot be so neatly defined when the word is used to translate terms in the New Testament. There was *ceremonial impurity* and *sensual impurity*, and the latter is indicated in this context. *Licentiousness* denotes an outrageous behavior, but the word "license," buried shallowly within our English word, can also be instructive at this point.

The next two works relate to pagan worship life. Transition is natural from adultery to *idolatry* and is often made in Scripture, both when they are separate acts and when the latter embraced or served as a spiritual form of the former. God created us in his image; idolatry is that practice by which we try to return the compliment. *Sorcery* refers to occult practices associated with idolatry, practices experiencing an alarming resurgence in our time.

The next eight vices belong together as fleshly works that supplant the ideal bond of love existing where the Spirit rules (Cf. v. 15) and are a veritable thicket of anti-social behaviors. The fourth and final group, *drunkenness* and *carousing*, belong together as intemperate sins that invoke excesses of degrading behavior. This was at least a second time that Paul had issued such warnings (v. 21), the previous one being on his earlier visit. His debarring of people who practiced such behavior from their inheritance of the kingdom did not conflict with justification by faith but merely defined the kind of faith that brings justification.

For Paul to have carried over his word "works" from his discussion of flesh to that of Spirit would have made a mismatch that limped all over the page. The Spirit has life inherent in itself in a way that flesh could never have. The notion of dead flesh makes much sense in a way that dead Spirit does not. When flesh dominates, there is a work performed on the person's part commensurate with wages (Rom 6:23) that must be forthcoming. When Spirit dominates, fruit is forthcoming that all fleshly effort could never produce were it not for the Spirit that animates us.

The plural, "fruits," would have been inappropriate because of the oneness that corresponds to the unitary Spirit, its producer. Some have translated the word "harvest" to catch the unitary thrust. But it is not the same as the word "reap" in 6:7ff. Fruit owes its oneness not only to the unitary character of the Spirit but to the inclusive effect of love, the first of the fruit. Just as there was no negative vice that corresponds to love as a positive virtue (Cf. v. 15), neither is there another virtue that gathers so much moral goodness into its sweep. Love is such that as a law it serves as a summation of all others; as a fruit, it must be inclusive of all others. It is first, yet more than a first among equals. If what we have here is a still-life sketch of a cornucopia of fruit, love so dominates the scene as to make all other members of the list honored to be there in their supporting roles.

To complement the unity of spiritual fruit, there is also a diversity. So we must also reckon with the fact that love stands alongside, albeit at the head of the line, of eight other fruitful virtues. The love here extolled is neither primarily an attitude, nor is it conditioned on being reciprocated by another. It is conditioned upon nothing and manages to express itself in deeds even if good feelings are hard to come by. To hear it best described one can turn to 1 Corinthians 13; to see it best exemplified, to Jesus Christ.

Joy flows freely from love and, like love, is independent of outward circumstance. It ran the gamut in the apostle's life from prosperity to persecution, from pulpit to prison.

Peace, to which we are introduced at the start of the letter (1:3), was a common greeting but, more than that, the fullness of well-being in both its personal and interpersonal expression.

Patience—literally long-temperedness—can be best grasped when we think of the havoc wrought upon our personal tranquility and social serenity by its opposite, short-temperedness.

Kindness would appear to be more commensurate with the attitudinal dimension of love, and yet it does not rule out severity when called for in other circumstances.

Generosity, often translated goodness, seems to describe the openness to others that is denied when we are stingy, be it with material benefits or brimming good will.

Faithfulness—literally faith—as a virtue, is more than the trusting response by which we are justified. It is fidelity, the side of faith that is often lost in our tendency to belittle its role in moral excellence.

Gentleness is the same as the meekness of the third beatitude (Matt 5:5). It includes the notions of teachableness and controlled strength.

Self-control denotes the aspect of the Spirit's dominance in our lives by which the flesh and its desires are restrained. If there is no law by which these things can be accomplished, neither is there a law to prohibit them (v. 23b).

Although flesh and Spirit represent a choice when the question of dominance is in focus, this does not mean that they cannot vie in the same life. What of this struggle between them in the life of the Christian? Paul's answer was that belonging to Christ is tantamount to crucifying the flesh. This is the second of three times that Paul mentioned the death of the Christian on the cross (Cf. 6:14). All three refer to this event as a past event.

The present reference is the only one of the three that moves beyond Paul's experience and generalizes to include all Christians. "Those who belong to Christ Jesus have crucified the flesh with its passions and desires" (v. 24). Not only do all Christians experience this death; they do so at their own hands. The secret of living by the Spirit is crucifying the flesh so that we no longer live by it although we live in it (2:20). Contrariwise, we live "by the Spirit" (5:25) and "by faith in the Son of God" (2:20).

Then Paul made a peculiar distinction: "If we live by the Spirit, let us also be guided by the Spirit" (v. 25). It is reminiscent of Galatians 5:1: "For freedom Christ has set us free." We have become free so that we can be free. Now we have become spiritual so that we can be spiritual. Paul used a different verb here (*zōmen*) from the one he used when he earlier told his readers to "live (*peripateite*) by the Spirit" (v. 16). The verb in the earlier passage is one that is large enough to embrace both the activities of living and being guided by. Here, in a more specialized sense, he distinguished between the two activities: "If it is the Spirit that animates us, let us be so guided." The indicative of living by the Spirit must be supplemented by the imperative of our being guided by the Spirit. The Spirit is our source of life; let the Spirit also give guidance and provide us with a sense of direction!

We earlier observed that the best that prohibitions can do pales into blandness when the prohibitions follow upon the heels of exalted and positive appeals. When Paul appealed to the great command of love (5:14), practical necessity mandated that he scold their pettiness because they had fallen so far short of love (5:15). Then as he appealed to the life and light of the Spirit, something about their present situation required him to say plainly: "Let us not become conceited, competing against one another, envying one another" (v. 26).

The Law of Maturity (6:1–6)

There is a unity in the opening verses of Galatians 6, although a looser one than in the other three passages being studied. We take verses 1-6 as a third reminder that freedom in Christ cannot mean lawlessness, and we see the unifying theme as that of Christian maturity. It thus takes its place alongside the law of love (5:13-15) and the life of the Spirit (5:16-26) as the law of maturity and a third impediment to lawlessness.

Paul, who spoke of his readers above as "those who belong to Christ" (5:24), here addresseed them as "you who have received the Spirit" (v. 1). Although the law of maturity is now in focus, the life of the Spirit continues to pervade all. Note also the shift from third person to second person, from generality to a concrete specific that addressed the readers. The specific situation involved an instance of someone being detected in a transgression. The element of surprise in "detected" could relate as easily to the transgressor as to the detector. The preposition preceding "transgression" could be translated "by" or "in." If "by," then the verb would best be translated "overtaken"; if "in," the verb is best translated "detected." The active agent of overtaking in the first case would be the transgression; in the second case, the detectors would be other people who found themselves in a position to either hurt or harm the victim. A good number of translators follow each option.

You can tell a lot about persons by the way they respond to such instances in the lives of others. The response that is approved and enjoined is that of restoration "in the spirit of gentleness." Gentleness is found among the fruit of the Spirit (5:23) and is thus an appropriate response to those "who have received the Spirit."

Romans 15:1 can be used as something of a bridge between the first two verses. It reads: "We who are strong ought to bear with the failings of the weak, and not to please ourselves." The injunction is quite different, but the same verb for "bear" is used there and in verse 2. "Bear" in both cases more likely means, not a matter of tolerantly putting up with, but of creatively and redemptively standing alongside. "Bear one another's burdens" is a paradigm instance of loving another; loving another is "the law of Christ" (v. 2). Since the law of Christ is fulfilled in one commandment, as is bearing another's burden, its connection with the command of love is unmistakable (5:14).

What greater spectacle is there of people who have unduly high opinions of themselvses than this: that of exploiting the moral failure of others for purposes of self-aggrandizement and not as an opportunity for helpful restoration? Indeed such persons, while thinking themselves to be something when they are really nothing, are thus self-deceived. "Nothing" often parades itself as "something," but all moral achievement is really the fruit of the Spirit within. And the Spirit obviously does not bear fruit in those people who parade without a permit!

One of the shoddiest and most self-deluding ways of acquiring a sense of self-worth is that which seeks a favorable comparison of oneself with people of moral failure. Indeed is this not the dynamic behind much gossip about others, whether it be true, false, or mixed? It has sometimes been called building up oneself by tearing down another. Surely such people need a good dose of "but for the grace of God, there go I!" That is the effect of the reminder to "take care that you yourselves are not tempted" (v. 1a).

To the contrary, it must be through a favorable testing of one's own works—as opposed to an unfavorable testing of another's works—that any sense of pride/ boasting can be forthcoming (v. 4). But Paul was a bit hypothetical and perhaps facetious here. Later he would claim to boast in nothing himself except "the cross of our Lord Jesus Christ" (v. 15). If Paul was really indicating that good within us may stand such a test, any pride or boastfulness in ourselves would certainly be misplaced, since it is the work of the Spirit!

Paul's reminder that "all must carry their own loads" (v. 5; i. e., in this matter of testing?) seems like a contradiction to verse 2. The fact that Paul used separate nouns for "burden" (v. 2) and "load" (v. 5) can relieve the conflict only in part. The former is a more generic word, while the latter suggests a "pack" of a more temporary duration. It does not seem inappropriate to compare Paul's idealism in verse 5 with adjustments we are often called to make for the world of realism, as in verse 2. Ideally, all should bear their own loads, but in the concrete situation of reality where this often does not happen, we show our maturity when we can find a place also for a part of the load of our brother or sister. In other words, there are times when love enjoins us to make someone else's load a part of our own. Thus burden-bearing is sometimes burden-sharing.

Verse 6 seems somewhat supended between the two longer passages. But it is best, as structure goes, to take it here as an example of sharing another's load. The example is that of religious "teachers." It is not clear whether these are teachers indigenous to the church or itinerate teachers who moved about. But the instruction would seem to apply in either and thus both cases. Paul elsewhere said that these teachers were entitled to material support (1 Cor 9:9-12a, 13-14), but he often forewent this right in his own case so as to enhance his witness (1 Cor 9:12b, 15-18; 1 Thes 2:9). On the other hand, there is no reason to limit "all good things" to material support. Its universal character demands that it and other non-material supports be forthcoming from the beneficiaries of ministry.

The Law of the Harvest (6:7–10)

To be freed from the law by Christ's crucifixion (2:19) and from the dictates of the flesh by our own self-crucifixion (5:24) does not mean that we are free from the law of the harvest. Anyone so interpreting the Christian's freedom has certainly misinterpreted it. Of this Paul was determined to remind his readers before he closed his letter.

This is the second time on the same page that Paul spoke of self-deception, although using differing verbs to do so. The first time had to do with an unjustified and inflated ground of self-worth (v. 3). Here he warned against the self-deception by which people convince themselves that God can be mocked by our indiscriminate sowing. To the contrary, whatever is sown must be reaped by the person doing the sowing (v. 7b).

This may be bad new, or it may be good news. The conflict between flesh and Spirit comes into play again. Unfortunately, the ones sowing to the flesh—see the works of the flesh above (5:19-21)—will have to reap the corruption they have sown (v. 8a). Indeed they reap the same quality of harvest, but in quantity, as with real life, immeasureably more. We sow the wind but reap the whirlwind (Hos 8:7).

Fortunately, the sowers to the Spirit—see the fruit of the Spirit above (5:22-23)—will get to reap what they have sown: the harvest of eternal life. And this fruit comes not just at the end of the growing season but can also grace our tables in the midst of that season. This is to say that eternal life is an ongoing reality for the believer and not something that merely awaits us at the end.

This double truth should serve as both an incentive and a disincentive to the weary one—an incentive despite weariness to keep sowing the seeds of the Holy Spirit to eternal life; a disincentive from sowing the harvest of corruption that sprouts from seeds of the flesh. Our good harvest is assured only when growing weary does not lead to giving up (v. 9).

We were earlier warned of "an opportunity" to be shunned, that to self-indulgence (5:13). Here is "an opportunity" (*kairon*, a time pregnant with possibility) to do good, thus sowing seed for the harvest of eternal life. All such seed need to be sown, but some are more pressing than others. We should do good to all but have a special duty to those of the "family of faith" (v. 10). Why so? The clue is to be found in Paul's use of a noun as the object of our doing good, viz., our spiritual household or "family of faith" (v. 10). Is it because those who will not provide for their own families (spiritual or other-wise) "have denied the faith and are worse than an unbeliever" (1 Tim 5:8)?

Conclusion

So Christian freedom is not only consistent with a positive morality; it entails it! A negative morality, so often associated with law, gives directives that, when violated, constitute sins of commission. A positive morality, nurtured by love, the Holy Spirit, the process of Christian maturation, and an awareness of an inevitable and consistent harvest, entails responsibilities that, when violated, constitute sins of omission. Although Christian morality does not preclude the need to observe the prohibitions of an authentic negative morality but everywhere enjoins it, the emphasis must ever be on the positive morality of observing the things that our Lord commanded (Matt 28: 20) and that his Spirit enables. Else, as later Pauline correspondence clarifies, we will be left naked, for we merely put off the old and fail to put on the new (Cf. Col 3:5-14; Eph 4:22-32) as depicted in Christian baptism (Rom 6:1-14). The negative morality of sweeping and tidying our house is simply ineffectual if we fail in the positive presence of a new Spirit (Luke 11: 24-26)!

Notes

[1]New Revised Standard Version (Iowa Falls IA: World Bible Publishers, Inc., 1989). Unless otherwise indicated all biblical texts cited will be from NRSV.

[2]Erich Fromm, *Escape from Freedom* (New York and Toronto: Farrar and Rinehart, Inc., 1941) 32-35.

[3]Cited in Amitai Etzioni, *The Hard Way to Peace* (New York: Collier Books, 1962) 110.

Responsible Freedom

Galatians 5:13-16

John B. Polhill

"Freedom"—in many ways this has been the watchword of our century. We fought two world wars to make the world "safe for democracy" and to free nations from aggressors. We have seen the breakup of great empires and the burgeoning of new independent nations—in Africa, in Asia, in the Caribbean. This has not always been with full succes, and many peoples have simply exchanged a slavery to foreign powers for enslavement to local despots. We have seen the breakup of the communist bloc in eastern Europe. I recently visited Russia. Not everyone there is wholly enamored of their new-found freedom. Some would like to return to the old regime. For them, freedom has not seemed all it was cracked up to be. It was easier to live as slaves of the state where others told you what to do and provided for your basic needs.

The cry for freedom has not been confined to the realm of nations. One finds it with many groups as well. It seems to have gained particular momentum in our country in the 1950s with the Civil Rights movement, summed up in Martin Luther King, Jr.'s famous vision of his people becoming "free at last." By the 1960s nearly every conceivable group with a real or imagined feeling of repression was crying for freedom. Those of us who were teachers felt it in our classrooms where students cried out for greater freedom, rebelling against any and all would-be voices of authority. I know of one incident where students stomped the floor so loudly with their feet that the professor had to evacuate the classroom.

All sorts of groups demanded their rights, their full freedom. The moral libertines formed a sexual freedom movement and protested what they saw as repressive laws governing sexual behavior. The women's liberation movement advocated equal rights and opportunities for women in the work force. Homosexuals came out of the closet demanding recognition of their lifestyle and their full and equal rights. With the draft protests in the 1960s, there were especially radical "freedom" movements that bordered on total anarchy, groups like Jerry Ruben's "yippies."

My purpose here is not to give an opinion on the merits and demerits of these movements. Obviously some represented serious grievances. Others are or were socially and politically naive. Others, from a Christian perspective, were simply immoral. The main point is that everyone seems to be longing for "freedom."

Now, this is a major theme of Galatians. Before Paul had come to the Galatians with the liberating gospel about Jesus, they had known what bondage was. They had been enslaved in the bondage of pagan idolatry, worshiping the unseen forces of nature, subject to the whims of imagined gods, dominated by a sense of fate. But, they had been set free from the dominance of the old gods by the message of God's grace in Jesus Christ. And yet, having found a new freedom in Christ, they were once again in danger of surrendering that freedom to a new religious tyranny. Christian legalists —"Judaizers" the scholars call them—were seeking to persuade them that their simple faith in Christ was not enough to ensure their salvation. They needed as well to be circumcised and to live by the whole of the Jewish law to be saved. This included keeping all the Jewish holy days, living by the minute food laws—the whole bit.

Paul was faced with a dilemma. On the one side, there was the danger of this legalistic religion with which the Judaizers were seeking to enslave the Galatians. Such legalism is the *opposite* of grace. On the other hand, there was the danger that some people would take the message of salvation by grace alone as a license to live a morally indifferent lifestyle. This is libertinism, and it is the *distortion* of grace. Paul had to walk the narrow line between both these aberrations and maintain a gospel rooted in grace alone but a gospel that resulted in moral responsibility. The whole of Galatians deals with this dilemma. It is the dilemma of Christian freedom. What does Paul say about freedom in Galatians?

(1) *Paul first of all makes it clear that mere self-centered freedom-seeking is an illusion. It is self-defeating and dangerous.*

Paul warned the Galatians that their freedom must not turn into an "opportunity for the flesh" ((5:13). For Paul, the "flesh" meant not so much the literal, physical flesh but rather the self-directed, selfish nature of people. To live "according to the flesh" is to live apart from God, to live with your eyes directed below on the things of this world rather than above on God. Paul realized that his message of freedom could be distorted into license for self-indulgence. He also realized that this would ultimately result in a new slavery —a slavery to oneself and one's own desires.

A little freedom can indeed be a dangerous thing. Henrietta hamster epitomized this principle. Henrietta was the pet hamster of the children of Paul Simmons, one of my seminary colleagues. My children were taking care of her while the Simmonses were away on vacation. The Simmonses warned us to keep Henrietta tightly caged: she liked her freedom and was an accomplished escape artist. Sure enough, we hadn't had her very long when the inevitable happened. We found her cage empty one morning. But scarcely had we discovered the tragedy when we heard a scratching noise coming from the children's bathroom. The noise led us to the wastepaper basket in their bathroom. Henrietta was trapped inside, trying desperately to scale its slippery sides, but to no avail. She was unharmed and soon safely back in her cage with a new supply of hamster food.

My wife and I returned to the kid's bathroom to try to reconstruct Henrietta's night of debauchery. How in the world did she find her way into the wastepaper basket? There was only one possible route that would have taken her there—from the bath-tub, across the towel rack to the top of the toilet. The wastepaper basket rested next to the toilet. Henrietta must have jumped from the toilet tank and landed in the basket. Had she jumped just slightly more to the left, she would have wound up in the toilet bowl and inevitable death by drowning. Henrietta's reckless night of freedom well-nigh claimed her life.

Freedom can be destructive for humans. I well remember the testimony of a young patient I met in the women's cirrhosis ward in Louisville's General Hospital. She had come from Chicago, the daughter of a strict Baptist preacher who kept her tightly reined. At sixteen she had decided to find her freedom and ran away from home. She ended up in Louisville and soon was into it all—sex, drugs, alcohol. Now she was in the hospital, suffering terribly from her alcohol addiction. "What promised me pleasure brought me pain," she said. "What promised me freedom made me its slave."

And what is true for individuals is just as true on the collective level. Freedom can be socially destructive. Paul accused the Galatians of "biting and devouring" one another (3:15). The difficulty so often in our quests for freedom is that they can be insensitive or indifferent to the rights and freedoms of others. Some militants advocate robbery, rape, and murder to further their cause and obtain their freedom. A father comes "out of the closet" and joins the gay community, abandoning his wife and children. What about the family's rights? These things happen, and they can happen in the supposed name of freedom.

In short, self-centered human striving for freedom can be self-defeating. All too often it self-destructs or leads to the destruction of others. Obviously, this kind of freedom is not the freedom Paul advocated.

(2) *Paul was not speaking about a freedom rooted in self but a freedom grounded in Christ.*

Paul was speaking of the freedom of grace. So, he spoke of love, loving your neighbor as yourself (3:14), fulfilling the royal law of love, loving as God in Christ has loved you. This is freedom, the freedom that comes from God in Christ, God's grace, Christ, the truth that sets us free.

The freedom that Christ gives us, the freedom of knowing your sins are forgiven and that your life is hidden in Jesus—that is the only true freedom there is. It began with creation. God gave human beings freedom, God's own freedom God gave to us. God gave us choice, the freedom to choose. But, this freedom of choice bears a risk: we can choose either to follow God's leading or to go our own way. When we choose the latter, we inevitably find ourselves culminating in that selfish, self-destructive cycle we have been describing. But, when we find the will of our creator and follow that, there we find our true freedom—the freedom to live life to the fullest, guided by the love of our creator, who wants what is best and most fulfilling for us.

Yet how does one find the will of the creator? We find it *in Christ*, the fullest revelation of God ever given. To grasp God's forgiveness and love in Christ is freedom indeed, freedom from self, freedom from sin, freedom from death, freedom to relate to all creation on the fullest level.

The Galatians had found this freedom in Christ. No longer were they enslaved to the fatalism of their old religion with its bondage to unseen powers. No longer did they face an uncertain future in the faith of fickle nature gods. They had the freedom of an assured salvation in Jesus Christ, of a new life directed by God, of a new being in the sphere of God's spirit and love.

All Christians who in faith have entrusted their lives to Christ have found freedom. It was so with the old Igorot woman some missionaries introduced me to in the Philippines. She had grown up with the same sort of animistic nature-religion the Galatians had once espoused. She showed me a hollow stick that she described as a "witch stick." When waved, it made a whistling noise—to ward off the woodland spirits, she was told as a girl. She symbolically tossed it to the ground. "I don't need it anymore," she said, "now I have Jesus." Yes, now she was free of the forest demons. She was free in Christ.

You who never believed in forest demons—you are also free. You are free from the fatalisms and bondages of an all-too-often callous modern world. You don't owe your soul to the company store, not even to the dollar. Your ultimate well-being does not depend on the stability of the institution you work for or the integrity of the local and national governments. You belong to Christ. You are free in him.

(3) *We are free in Christ, but there is a limit to this freedom. Freedom in Christ is never license. It is "responsible freedom."*

We are now freed from our self-seeking. We are freed from self and free to live a life that is pleasing to God. In Paul's words, we are freed from the "flesh"; we are no longer enslaved to a life bound by sin and self.

It is a seeming paradox but a profound truth. We find true freedom when we become slaves of Christ. True freedom is to bind ourselves to Christ and the leading of his Spirit. Only by binding ourselves to Christ are we freed from an inevitable bondage to sin and self-seeking.

Self-seeking is indeed sin at its deepest level. When we see ourselves as masters of our own destiny, we put ourselves in the place of God. We delude ourselves into thinking that we are really free, free to choose our own way. But, it *is* a delusion. As we have seen, that sort of freedom is self-destructive. Every parent knows that. A child simply cannot handle total freedom. The child must be given limits, boundaries, rules. I grew up with a boy whose parents set few rules for him. His mother wanted to do nothing to stifle his "creativity." He was indeed precocious but a total social misfit. He could not relate to anyone and ended up a total failure in life. He ended life at his own hand in his early twenties.

No, true freedom is not an absolute, self-directed freedom. It is responsible freedom, freedom within limits, freedom from one's own misdirected desires. The ultimate source of this freedom is found in Jesus Christ. When we bind ourselves to Christ and the direction of his Spirit, we are truly free to live life to the very fullest that God created us to live.

And, what is true of individuals is also true in our relationships to others. Christian freedom means a new openness to, a new responsibility toward others. Freed from our own self-centeredness, we are now free to relate to others. Thus in Galatians 5:13, when speaking of freedom in Christ, Paul quickly moved on to talk of loving one another and serving one another. Christian freedom is not a license to fulfill one's own desires and ego needs. It is a release from these in order that we might love and serve others.

The difficulty with most human striving for freedom is that it never really overcomes the dimension of human selfishness. We must have *our* way, and in the seeking for this freedom we often tread on the rights and freedom of others. In Christ, we learn to esteem others, to love others, to serve others. And they, in response, are more likely to acknowledge our freedom as well as find their own in Christ.

It isn't easy. The Christian life is never easy. We will encounter those persons along the way who will not acknowledge our freedom and who will rebuff our attempts at love and reconciliation. There is only one certainty that will keep us going: no matter what our status by this world's standards, we are *free* in Christ. We must live out this freedom consistently, selflessly, *responsibly* in the hope that those around us will see our freedom, acknowledge our freedom, and want our freedom for themselves.

Freedom in Christ is freedom indeed. The world is full of bondages. It longs to be free. We have the liberating gospel. We must proclaim it and live it out responsibly in our own lives that others might also know the true freedom that comes when we bind ourselves to Christ.

Land of the Free

Galatians 5:13-15

C. Alan Melton

The Fourth of July—what on earth has that to do with the church? What *does* the Fourth of July have to do with *religion* at all? If churches are going to celebrate the Fourth of July during Sunday worship, then shouldn't it have something to do with religion? But does it? Certainly it does.

Many persons, of course, think that the Fourth of July has a great deal to do with religion. They would almost equate the birthday of America with the birthday of Israel. Some wish to think that America is the new Israel, that America is the long awaited promised land. My personal feeling is that this is a misreading of Scripture to think that any country is God's chosen instrument for the redemption of the world. Israel didn't even do very well in that role. It is a misuse of the Old Testament to see the nation of Israel now as the nation of America. It leaves out the New Testament that clearly says that it is not the nation any longer but the church that is the new Israel.

So for me, our country's birthday is not the birthday of the new Israel or the birthday of the Christian nation of the world. No, it's the Fourth of July—the birthday of the United States of America, the birthday of our great and wonderful and very free democracy that we are all privileged today to call home.

I.

But a *democracy* is different from a *theocracy*. Israel was a theocracy. *Theos* in Greek means God. Israel was a *God*-ruled, *God*-led nation. We are a democracy. *Demos* means people. We are a *people*-led nation. The difference makes all the difference in the world. Israel understood itself to be ruled by God. Later on Israel had kings who ruled it, but the kings were not elected "for the people, by the people, of the people." They were anointed by God, and they ruled as God told them to rule. Israel had no concept of a nation being led by normal, regular, and frail human persons. It was a theocracy, God's nation, and it believed that God directed it as God wished through God's own chosen agents—a very different form of government and understanding of religion from what we have today. We are a "modern" democracy, a concept that wasn't even conceived until the fifteenth century. The Enlightenment helped the world to see that you could have government of the people, by the people, and for the people. This is very different from the theocracy of Israel thousands of years ago.

Now if we want to change America into a theocracy, then we can all get together and go to the polls and do that. Some Christians, in fact, want to do exactly that. They call themselves the Christian Reconstruction Movement, and Pat Robertson is one of their main leaders. If we want to go that route, we are free to do so. We can replace the Constitution of the United States with the Ten Commandments and let the Ten Commandments be the law of the land instead of the Constitution. That's what they mean when they say they want to "reconstruct" America. We can have a theocracy if we choose to have one. But before we go that route we should remember what James Dunn loves to say: "The only problem with a *theo*cracy is that everybody wants to be 'theo!' "

At least in a democracy a bunch of people make the decisions, not one, self-appointed or God-appointed, divine king. Now I understand why some people think we need to go that route. It would be a lot simpler. But when it comes down to the choice of the

America that we have—this wonderful, free democracy—or a theocracy that only allows one certain brand of "Christian" religion, I will remain a conservative and vote for us to stay as we are now.

Because we are not a theocracy, we are also not a "Christian nation," in the strictest sense of the term. But we are a nation made up largely of many Christians. About ninety percent of the population would say they believe in God, in a personal God. We are a nation of religious persons. But we are not strictly a formal, religious nation. We are not a theocracy or a "Christian nation." We are a democracy, a nation where many persons happen also to be Christian. Because so many of us are Christians and because this has been true since the beginning of our nation much of our government has been influenced by Christian beliefs, values, and understandings of life. These were written into the very fabric of our founding documents.

Many of our founders were practicing Christians, and they remained so. But they were smart Christians. In this wonderful experiment in democracy, even though they were Christians, they did not create a land where everybody else had to be a Christian. Isn't that wonderful? Nor did they say that only Christians could have the rights of citizenship or that only Christians deserved to lead the nation. They created "one nation under God," but this God was the great creator God, and under this God there was much, much room for freedom of worship and diversity. One could be a Congregationalist, a Baptist, a Catholic, or a Presbyterian. You could even be Jewish. You could even choose not to be religious at all and still be treated with equality. That was the freedom envisioned for this democracy in this land of the free.

So the founders created a nation where persons could freely worship as they pleased without fear of persecution by the state. It was a great, grand, glorious, and wonderful new experiment, this government—because it wasn't that way in England. It wasn't that way in Virginia either, by the way, nor in Massachusetts in the early days, not until James Madison and John Leland insisted that we have religious freedom in this country. Many of the people who first came here thought, "No, let's have a state religion." In Virginia it was the Episcopal Church that was the state religion. In some of the northern colonies it was the Congregational Church that the residents had to support with their tax money. The Puritans wanted their religion to be the official religion. They wanted to eliminate other religious groups and on some occasions did—as when they burned "witches."

But we need to read on in the next chapter of history and not stop with those earliest colonists because those folks did not win out in the long run. They wanted one religion, one kind of Christianity, in the nation, but they lost. James Madison and John Leland —the Baptist preacher who had been locked up in jail in Culpepper, Virginia, for preaching without a license—helped to get religious freedom written into the Constitution. They convinced the founders that there should be no establishment of one religion, but that all faiths would be free from government intrusion.

This is our land of the free, this wonderful American experiment—the only nation in the world to establish the separation of church and state that allows for pluralism and diversity and freedom for everyone, even those who do not choose to be religious. I don't know about you, but when you ask me what I love about America, I love that. In this country I am free to worship God as I so choose.

Even the Southern Baptist Convention will not give us that much freedom. The country allows us more freedom than some of our own forebears. I don't know about you, but I am grateful to live in a country that allows me to worship God as I see fit or even not to worship God if I also see fit.

II.

But we cannot judge the forebears by present-day standards. This is 1994, not 1776. Many things have changed in our country. They created a country where people could be free to worship. Most of the people were either Protestants, Catholics, or Jews.

There were a few other religions in America in 1776, but not many at all. Now we live in a very different world. We have Muslims in our country today . . . Buddhists . . . Hindus . . . Christian Scientists . . . Seventh Day Adventists . . . Mormons. We have all kinds of religious people in our country. Are we to squelch all of these other religions and allow diversity only among the Christians? Will we also let Muslim persons pray at the football games? Many of us may not have thought about that because many of us don't have any Muslim persons in our town who would ask to pray at football games. But if we lived in Washington D.C. or some other large city, we would. Should our Jewish children have to tolerate Christian baccalaureate services? Maybe no one has raised a fuss about this in your town, but surely even in your town not everyone is a Protestant Christian. We live in a nation now that is made up not only of many Christians but of religious people of all kinds of faith.

As I understand the Constitution and the Bible, the people of other religions too must have religious liberty and freedom to worship God as they choose. As I understand the Constitution and the Scriptures, every person in our land is free to worship God as that person sees fit, regardless of how they might see God or how they might choose to worship. We may not like that. We may want to change them, and we have the right to try to convert Hindus and Buddhists to the Christian faith if we choose. But unless we want to change the Constitution, we don't have a right to change our country from a democracy to a theocracy.

Again, it is important to remember the difference between democracy and theocracy. There is something tricky about freedom. As long as everybody in the country is free to worship God as they so choose, then you and I also remain free to worship God as we so choose. But the day someone—anyone—cannot worship God as they choose, then the next day they may decide that you and I cannot worship God as we so choose. If I have learned anything at all about faith and life, it is this: Freedom for all ensures freedom for all. Freedom for some ensures freedom only for some.

III.

To be free, you and I are going to have to become a little more tolerant. This will not be easy for us to do. I must confess that I didn't say anything to my own ministerial colleagues this year when I was on the committee that planned the baccalaureate service. But I did at least think about it. I wondered how the Jewish kids would feel. I wondered how the Mormons would feel or the Seventh day Adventists, or the Christian Scientists, or other religious groups. Now, of course, the non-religious children don't have to come to the baccalaureate service, but I wondered about the fairness of that too. Certainly the service was not sponsored by the school and was not, therefore, sponsored by the government. And we Baptists feel good about that. Such services never should have been government sponsored to begin with, not if we really believe in the separation of church and state. I feel good that it was the ministerial association that planned the service. But should we have one for other faiths? Should there have been one for Jews, Muslims, Mormons, and Seventh Day Adventists?

This land of the free is not as easy as it use to be in 1776. But we are all called to be responsible Christian persons, to make sure that this land of the free is the land of the free for every citizen, especially in the area of religion. That's our specialty. So, personally I hope we never become a theocracy and that we always continue to be this wonderful, free democracy that we have been since our founders had their dreams. For I love this great American country of ours.

I know some of those persons who want to be "theo." If they run the country, it won't just be the Muslims and Jews who won't have any religious liberty. Neither will you and I. Freedom for all protects freedom for all. Freedom for some protects freedom for only some.

There is a country and western tune that reads like this: "I'm proud to be an American, where at least I know I'm free." There is a text in Galatians that says: "For you were called to freedom, brothers and sisters; only do not use your freedom as an opportunity for self-indulgence, but through love become slaves to one another, for the whole law is summed up in a single commandment: 'You shall love your neighbor as yourself.' " I would add that freedom for your neighbor should be as important as freedom for yourself. "If, however," Paul wrote, "you bite and devour one another, take care that you are not then consumed by one another."

Freedom of religion means freedom for all persons to worship God as they see fit—even if it is not our God and even if it is not as we see fit. That's still what this great nation of ours is about, this land of the free. I personally hope we keep it that way, because that's why I am proud to be an American and a Christian. And that's why I am happy to celebrate our nation's birthday, for it lets me and everyone around me be religiously free.

Weaving the Fabric of Community

Galatians 5:22-26

Kate Penfield

Prayer

Let us begin our meditation as we begin our lives, centered on the basic truths of our faith story, praying together for reconciliation.

Leader: "The Lord God said, 'It it not good that a human being should be alone. . . .' " (Gen 1:18)

People: **Gracious God, we thank you for our story of origin that calls us to partnership in order to be complete.**

Leader: "Then I looked and I heard the voice of many angels surrounding the throne and the living creatures and the elders; they numbered myriads of myriads and thousands of thousands, singing together with full voice; and every creature in heaven and on earth and under the earth and in the sea, and all that is in them, singing." (Rev 5:11, 13)

People: **Even more do we thank you for our story of destiny that summons us to a multi-cultural, multi-hued, multi-dimensional weaving of all that is into one harmonious whole.**

Leader: Yet "when people began to multiply on the face of the ground . . . the Lord God saw that the wickedness of humankind was great on the earth, and that every inclination of their thoughts was only evil continually, . . . and it grieved God to the heart." (Gen 6:1, 5, 6)

People: **But in between where we come from and where we are going, we confess that we are caught in the confines of the human condition, between the will to partnership with and the will to power over, and community is torn asunder.**

Leader: "In Christ all things hold together . . . and you who were once estranged and hostile in mind, doing evil deeds, Christ has now reconciled in his fleshly body through death. . . ." (Col 1:17, 21-22)

People: **We thank you that also with us in the in between is Jesus Christ, whose cross is the link between creation and consummation, opening to us a new way of being together.**

Leader: "As many of you as were baptized into Christ have clothed yourselves with Christ. There is no longer Jew or Greek, there is no longer slave or free, there is no longer male and female; for you are all one in Christ Jesus . . . heirs according to the promise." (Gal 3:28-29)

People: **And we thank you that the Holy Spirit, knowing that we are lineal, sequential thinkers, is dealing with us slowly, inexorably, one issue at a time, to weave us into one glorious whole.**

Unison: **Lord our God, we thank you that we are here and now with these our sisters and brothers. Stretch us as Christ was stretched on the cross to hold things together, until the strands of our separateness are woven together into the fabric of community that glorifies you. Amen.**

Meditation

The other day I was talking to a weaver whom I had invited to demonstrate his art at a First Baptist Church in America breakfast as we gathered for a new season in our life together. The theme selected for the season's worship and education was "Woven Together in Love"—how through the exchanges of the life we share we are woven ever more closely with God and with one another. To begin the series, it seemed appropriate to enrich our eating and talking and singing with an actual experience of the weaving we desire to experience in the community of our church.

The weaver had stationed his seven-foot loom in front of a window so that as he invited us to participate with him in the weaving and the project grew, we could observe our progress clearly outlined against the light. With all the elements of a new creation before us, the weaver described the wool yarn as handspun from the fleece of sheep; the process of finger weaving as the oldest and simplest method known; the product as a natural, beautiful, lightweight yet warm and strong covering. Then he proceeded with immense skill and patience not simply to create by himself, but to involve all who would come, of all ages and abilities, in the creation.

What a metaphor for God's way with humanity, inviting us into the weaving together of all our lives, where the basic materials of community joined by the oldest and simplest means produce shelter for ourselves and the world around us. Yet how often we get it wrong, and the ties that bind are unraveled.

We are caught in the confines of the human condition, spelled out in our story of origin, displayed in the news and in our own lives every day. On the one hand we yearn for partnership with our sisters and brothers, because in the depths of our beings resounds the truth that it is not good for human beings to be alone. On the other hand we want power over our sisters and brothers, tempting and trapping and passing the buck to get our own way in the clamor of special interest claims we bring to the table of life. Do you hear the echoes of the Genesis creation story in these words? More importantly, do you hear the echoes of our own lives?

This is where we live, caught in the conflict between the will to partnership with and the will to power over. How shall we ever reconcile these two interests? How will God weave together the polarities to create the fabric of community?

The key is in the way of Jesus Christ, whose cross is the crux of it all, we might say. A Carmelite abbess put it this way:

> What I love about the image of Christ crucified is that it seems to me that one of the biggest things in life is the tensions that pull us in a million directions. . . . And that's what the whole image of the crucifixion is for me—Christ stretched to every possible conceivable direction in the universe. Seemingly he's broken by that, but being broken by those tensions he emerges with a kind of wholeness and integration. Not by avoiding any of the extremes, not by avoiding any bit of the tension, but by absolutely moving into it and moving out of it.[1]

"All things hold together in Jesus Christ," wrote the apostle Paul in one letter, and in the letter to the Galatians he amplified, "As many of you as were baptized in Christ have clothed yourselves in Christ. There is no longer Jew or Greek, there is no longer slave or free, there is no longer male and female; for you are all one in Christ Jesus."

The Holy Spirit knows that we are lineal, sequential thinkers, and deals with us patiently, slowly, inexorably, one issue at a time, to remind us of what we see in Jesus Christ, that we are all one. Chronologically, in the time of Paul the issue of Judaizers was resolved to invite into Christianity people who had never been Jews. In the last century we began to work on the sin of racism, a task far from accomplished but never since abandoned. In this century we deal with manifestations of sexism. How long, O Lord? The reality is that we are one, and God will have our lives together reflect that truth as the threads of all our differences are caught up in one richly variegated whole.

Here is how: Also in Galatians Paul presented two lists set in opposition, the first detailing what he called sins of the flesh, which arise from that desire for power over the other and rip the fabric of community. "I am warning you," he said, "those who do such things will not inherit the kingdom of God."

But there is another list, another way of being together: "By contrast, the fruit of the Spirit is love, joy, peace, patience, kindness, generosity, faithfulness, gentleness, and self-control. . . . Those who belong to Christ Jesus have crucified the flesh with its passions and desires. If we live by the Spirit, let us walk by the Spirit. Let us not become conceited, competing against one another, envying one another."

The way of weaving our lives in partnership is the way of Jesus Christ, by entering directly into the issues and, yes, the evils, of our day, and right there in the midst of them growing the fruit of the Spirit in order to become whole. Notice that these characteristics that create and strengthen community are not instant givens, nor are they individual gifts; they are organic—fruit—that develop and mature over time as the product of our interactions together when we grapple with the difficult dynamics and decisions that confront any group, and they are for the sake of the whole.

Our story of destiny depicts concentric circles of all creation gathered as one circle of praise around God, a multidimensional weaving beyond our imagination, the reconciliation of all things, the kingdom of God that we both inherit and create. Here is the heart of what I believe about where we are headed, that we shall ultimately have with all creation what in this life we have only partially with only one person only if we are extremely blessed. Then, in that kingdom we are already creating here and now, all our loneliness will be wrapped up in face to face partnership with everything, and all our power will be for the sake of binding together.

Against the light of that goal we observe our progress. We see all the elements of the new creation: The Lamb Jesus Christ offering everything for this weaving, moving into and through the tensions of life epitomized by the cross, and clothing us in his ways. We see the oldest and simplest and surest methods known— love, joy, peace, patience, kindness, generosity, faithfulness, gentleness, and self-control—exercised by us with varying, ever maturing degrees of skill. We see the shelter of lives joined in circles of caring created by our hands, because the Master Weaver has given us everything it takes but has ultimately left the project in our hands.

Whenever I look at the product of our morning weaving experience in its triangular shape, I am reminded of God who is one yet is known to us as Father, Son and Holy Spirit joined in a community of love, one reality yet infinitely complex. When I look closer, in its intersecting threads are multiple crosses, sign of the reconciliation we are accomplishing in the name and the way of Jesus Christ, as we are stretched through the exchanges of our life together, until the strands of our separateness are woven together in the fabric of community that glorifies God.

Prayer

Let us end our meditation as we began, praying together for reconciliation:

Gracious God, give us the grace to see our stories through the light of Christ's story, and then to clothe ourselves in his ways and to walk in his Spirit, thereby weaving a fabric of community that shall warm and comfort all whose lives we touch; in the name of Jesus Christ. Amen.

Note

[1]Mother Tessa Bielecki in *The Search for Meaning: Americans Talk about What They Believe and Why*, ed. Phillip L. Berman (New York: Ballantine Books, 1990) 347.

Cramming[1]

Galatians 6:7-10

Robert G. Baker

When you were in school, did you ever "cram"? Did you ever stay up all night right before a big test or final exam, attempting to cram a huge amount of learning into your head before the next day? Most of us at one time or another in our student experiences have crammed. In his book *First Things First*, Stephen Covey admits that he did. He wrote about his experiences as follows:

> I'm ashamed to admit it, but I crammed my way through undergraduate school, thinking I was really clever. I learned to psych out the system, to figure out what the teacher wanted. "How does she grade? Mostly on lectures? Great! I don't have to worry about reading the textbook. What about this other class? We have to read the book? Okay, where are the Cliff Notes so I can get a quick summary instead?" I wanted the grade but I didn't want it to crimp my lifestyle.
>
> Then I got into graduate work, a different league altogether. I spent my first three months trying to cram to make up for four years of undergraduate cramming, and I wound up in the hospital with ulcerated colitis. I was trying to force the natural processes, and I found out that, long term, you simply can't do it. I spent years trying to compensate for the foolishness of getting myself into a value system that was not tied to principles at all.[2]

I can resonate with Covey. In college and graduate school, I was the "King of Crammers." I put off, postponed, and procrastinated. I learned the subtle art of studying for a grade. The night before a big test I would stay up all night forcing myself to "cram" all of the information into my head I would need to make an "A."

And make A's I did. Lots of them. All A's through college, seminary, and graduate school as a matter of fact. But if you were to ask me twenty-four hours after the test what I had learned, much of the information would have been forgotten. Crammed knowledge tends not to be lasting knowledge. We don't retain a healthy percentage of what we cram.

So I "crammed" and made the A's. I was known as a good student. But I would have attained a better education if I had possessed the discipline of studying daily and preparing along the way rather than just "cramming" it all in the night before the exam.

In retrospect, my "cramming" was crazy. Too many all nighters studying for tests and writing research papers eventually took their toll on me. I'd stay up all night, take the test or turn in the paper, and then be "shot" for the rest of the day. Often after the test when I needed to sleep and wanted to sleep, I couldn't sleep. There were other classes to attend. Besides, I usually had so much caffeine in my system from all night coffee-drinking that I couldn't relax.

Now, I could get by with my "cramming" for a day or two, but then final exams would arrive and I would attempt to pull four or five all-nighters in a row. I was a walking zombie, a real joy to be around. (Just ask my wife who celebrated more than I did when I finally finished school.) I needed to rest, but there was always more "cramming" to do.

It all came to a head for me one Sunday morning down at Midway Baptist Church in Midway, Kentucky. The week before had been finals week. Naturally, I had stayed up almost all week studying and cramming for tests and churning out research papers that had been assigned at the beginning of the semester. But in graduate school, I also was a pastor, and Sunday came every week (even during finals week). So I had stayed up late on Saturday night writing a sermon. I "crammed" for that sermon and attempted to preach it the next morning.

I still remember that sermon, not because of its content—which wasn't all that bad—but because of my delivery that day—which was terrible.

I preached that day from Matthew 7:12, the portion of Jesus' Sermon on the Mount known as the "Golden Rule." But my preaching was hardly golden. It wasn't even silver or bronze. Rusty was more like it. "Mush-mouthed" to be more precise.

"Do unto others as others do unto you," I proclaimed. "Do unto you as unto you others have done," I said. "Others unto you do as you have done," I declared. "Have done you others do so," I stated.

Any way that you could say the Golden Rule except the correct way was how I preached it that day. I stumbled and mumbled my way through that sermon. It was as if I was in a fog, and I know the members of my congregation were in a fog. Their bewildered expressions and blank stares confirmed what had happened. Finals week had taken its toll. Their preacher had pulled one all-nighter too many. "Cramming" had caught up with me.

I just wanted to forget that sermon. I never wanted to preach on Matthew 7:12 again. But every now and then when my wife wants to humble me just a little, all she has to say is: "Remember the Golden Rule sermon, Robert. Remember the Golden Rule!" Or— even if I have not been pleased with a sermon—she will say: "Well, at least it wasn't as bad as the Golden Rule."

Did you, as I did, ever "cram" in school? Do you, even if you are not out of school, still sometimes find yourself wanting the "grade" without crimping your lifestyle?

In the short-term, "cramming" may appear to work. But in the long run, "cramming" is an empty promise, a non-lasting quick fix. And it will take its toll on you. You may not—as Steven Covey— develop ulcerated colitis. You may not—as I did—become zombie-like or mush-mouthed as you preach on the "Rusty Rule." But eventually, if you continue to "cram," you will suffer consequences. No one is forever exempt. "Cramming" will indeed catch up with you!

Now opposed to "cramming" is the "Law of the Farm."[3] In scriptural terms, this principle might be called the "Agriculture of the Spirit." You can read about it in Galatians 6:7-10.[4]

What is the "Law of the Farm"? "In agriculture," writes Steven Covey, it is when "we can easily see and agree that natural laws and principles govern the work and determine the harvest."[5]

For example, most crops have a specified growing season. It takes a certain amount of time for a seed to germinate, grow, mature, and be ready for harvest. Within this growing season, there are certain tasks that need to be done at specified times if a productive crop is to be expected. These tasks include plowing, planting, watering, fertilizing, weeding, cultivating, and harvesting. Can you imagine what would happen if farmers tried to "cram" on the farm? If they attempted to short-circuit the growing season? If they—after postponing and procrastinating all year—tried to speed up the natural processes and still reap the harvest on time?

I was raised on a tobacco farm in Scott County, Kentucky. Each fall my father recruited me (and as many other workers as he could find) to help "cut and house" (harvest) his tobacco crop. This year Dad planned to begin harvesting his crop on Tuesday, August 30. Do you think he went out on the farm on Monday, August 29, and said: "I think it's time to plow this field, set this crop, fertilize, weed, and water the plants so that this crop will grow today and we can harvest it tomorrow"?

My dad would not expect his crop to grow and mature in one day. We would not expect that either. The "Law of the Farm" doesn't work that way. You've got to prepare well in advance. Certain tasks need to be done within specified time frames. "Cramming" doesn't work on the farm!

Yet, it's not just on the farm. There are actually many life situations where "cramming" doesn't work. Indeed, in contrast to "cramming," it is the "Law of the Farm" (the "Agriculture of the Spirit") that applies in most areas of life.

As we have already noted, "cramming" doesn't "cut it" in school. Oh, we might "cram" and get the degree. But we don't get the best education. We go to school with the illusion that we can sow one thing (like partying and extracurricular activities) and expect to reap another thing (like the ability to think analytically, to communicate creatively, and other lifelong benefits of our courses). We won't face the reality of long-term development and growth. But still, the "Law of the Farm" applies.

Then there is the area of health and physical fitness. Can you decide to get in shape, rent a Jane Fonda work-out video that night, watch it for an hour while you sit back in your Lazy-Boy recliner, and then expect to be in shape the next day? After years of a "junk-food-diet-little-or-no-exercise" lifestyle, can you expect to compete in a 5K or 10K run next week by joining a health club a few days before? It takes time, work, perseverance, and discipline to get in shape. The "Law of the Farm" applies.

My brother-in-law, Sam Simpson, is the head football coach at Henry Clay High School in Lexington, one of the largest high schools in Kentucky. Prior to his arrival as head coach, Henry Clay had lost nineteen straight football games. During his first season the team won six and lost four, just missing a berth in the play-offs. This year (Sam's second season) the team is off to a 4–0 start! Do you think Henry Clay's players showed up on Thursday before this season's opening Friday night game and said: "Coach," we think we'd like to have a football team. Could you teach us a few plays and help us decide who should play what positions? Coach, we think we're ready. We're going to open the season to-morrow night with a win"?

Of course, my brother-in-law's players didn't say that or do that. They underwent all kinds of preparation long before the Thursday prior to opening game. They lifted weights and ran in the off season. They played in "passing leagues" during the summer. They had long two-a-day practices beginning the first of August. They had to learn the playbook. They had to understand strategy. There were all the pre-season scrimmages and the mental and emo-tional preparation of learning to play as a team and of believing that they could be successful. And when it came time to play the opening game this year, they were ready. (They won 41 to 8!) How come? Because they in essence had dared to apply the "Law of the

Farm" in their preparation. They didn't try to "cram" all of their pre-season training into one day.

Don't set aside the "Law of the Farm" too quickly. It pertains to other vital areas as well. Consider marriage for a few moments. The "Law of the Farm" certainly is applicable. Couples with good marriages understand that it takes time to plant, nurture, cultivate, and grow seeds of love, caring, shared vision, and friendship. Yet, many couples simply do not give their marriage enough time.

The devotional writer, Oscar Green, has said that far too many couples try to cram marriage into a few days each year. Husbands seem especially prone to be ensnared by this trap. They try to cram love, devotion, and appreciation for their wives into three days: (1) her birthday; (2) their anniversary; and (3) Christmas![6] And woe be unto those husbands who forget one of those three days!

As a minister, I have counseled many married couples who want out of the relationship or who need help feeling better about staying in the relationship. Various dynamics are usually involved whenever a marital relationship goes awry. Yet, one dynamic that is often present in troubled, struggling marriages is a lack of time. Too little time is given to the nurturing and development of the relationship. Indeed, I know couples who devoted more time to their wedding than they have devoted to their marriage. A beautiful, well-orchestrated wedding is nice and even desirable. But if it comes down to a choice between a good wedding and a good marriage, I'll take a good marriage every time. You just cannot "cram" marriage into a one-time wedding celebration, a three-day-per-year recognition, or a "whenever-I-get-around-to-it" routine. "Cramming" doesn't result in a healthy marriage. The "Law of the Farm" applies.

Parenting is still another area where the "Law of the Farm" is relevant. There are no real shortcuts as far as responsibly raising children. Oh, there are those parents who try—attempting to shift the major responsibility for training their children onto churches, youth groups, schools, baby sitters, even to televisions and VCR's. But parents cannot expect to reap the results of happy, well-rounded children by just showing up every now and then to "cram" in a little love, discipline, and encouragement. Children need parents to be present. Good parenting can't be "crammed."

The "Law of the Farm" has an impact on your vocation. You can't goof off or fool around most of the time, "cram" in some work every now and then, and expect to be the best possible lawyer, minister, doctor, administrator, real estate agent, teacher, businessperson, or whatever your particular vocation happens to be. Sowing the seeds and reaping the harvest of a satisfying, successful vocation takes time.

School, physical fitness/health, sports, marriage, parenting, vocation—in each of these areas the "Law of the Farm" applies. And in each of these areas, "cramming" lurks as a "shortcut to satisfaction" temptation that—though often producing short-term success—eventually gives way to long-term consequences.

"Well, Bob," you say, "that's fine. What you have shared sounds like an introductory, motivational speech that you might expect to hear at Freshmen Orientation. But, Bob, why talk about "cramming" and the "Law of the Farm" during a Sunday morning worship service? Why incorporate these concepts in a sermon at all?"

My "answer" and "defense" would be that these techniques and approaches to life also affect our faith in Christ and our service through the church. In fact, the apostle Paul must have assuredly had something akin to the "Law of the Farm" in mind when he wrote the following:

> Do not be deceived; God is not mocked, for you reap whatever you sow. If you sow to your own flesh, you will reap corruption from the flesh; but if you sow to the Spirit, you will reap eternal life from the Spirit. So let us not grow weary in doing what is right, for we will reap at harvest time, if we do not give up. So then, whenever we have an opportunity, let us work for the good of all, and especially for those of the family of faith. (Gal 6:7-10)

The apostle Paul knew about "cramming" long before "cramming in college" was in vogue. He was aware of those who wanted a "quick-fix-cram-it-all-in-at-once-and-get-it-over-with" approach to religion. He knew about those Christians who wanted the "grade" (salvation) but who didn't want Christianity to crimp their lifestyle. The apostle discerned that Jesus didn't have "cramming" in mind when our Lord declared: "If any want to become my followers, let them deny themselves and take up their cross daily and follow me" (Luke 9:23).

"Cramming" won't "cut it" when it comes to being a fully devoted follower of Christ. But have you noticed? A lot of us Christians still try to "cram." If we are not careful, we will find ourselves trying to "cram" all of our religion and Christianity in on Sunday, or on Christmas, or at Easter, or during a revival. We will "cram it in" and "turn it on" when we're in trouble or when there's a crisis. But we won't devote enough time or give our faith enough time to grow, develop, and mature. We wonder why we don't harvest the fruit of the Spirit mentioned in Galatians 5:22: love, joy, peace, patience, kindness, generosity, faithfulness, gentleness, and self-control. It's because we don't practice the "Law of the Farm" mentioned in Galatians 6:7-10.

Listen, Christ did not come and give himself sacrificially so that we could just "cram" in a little religion whenever we are in trouble. Christ came so that we might have life and have it more abundantly.

But what's the solution to "cramming" in regard to our faith? How can we apply the "Law of the Farm" (the "Agriculture of the Spirit") to our individual lives and to the corporate life of our church? To provide some guidance in discovering the answers to these questions, I want to do two things: (1) tell you a story, and (2) provide you with a syllabus.

First, the story. It is the story of Tony Gwynn of the San Diego Padres. He is arguably the best and purest hitter in major league baseball today. During this past strike-shortened season, Tony Gwynn's batting average was an astounding .394 (he averaged 3.94

hits every ten times he went to the plate). Now that might not mean much to you if you are not a baseball fan, but .394 is the highest batting average for a season that any major league ball-player has had since 1941 when Ted Williams batted .406. In fact, no major leaguer has hit .400 since Williams' .406 fifty-three years ago.[7]

Could Tony Gwynn have accomplished such an amazing feat? Could he have hit .400 in 1994? I can't tell you for certain if he could have pulled it off or not, and now—because of the season-ending strike—we will not find out (at least this year). But I can tell you something for certain about Tony Gwynn, who is one of the most respected and personable players in all of baseball. When it comes to the art of hitting a baseball, Tony Gwynn believes in and puts into practice the "Law of the Farm." Allow me to explain.

Not only is Tony Gwynn a gifted hitter; he is also a meticulous, disciplined student of the game. On road trips, he takes along video equipment and has a clubhouse attendant tape every one of his "at-bats." Then, between games when other teammates are sleeping or out socializing, Tony edits those tapes by splicing together each of his "at-bats" against each pitcher he faces. Over the years he has produced a voluminous video file to which he often refers. When he learns who will be the starting opposing pitcher for the next game, Tony watches all of his previous at-bats against that par-ticular pitcher. Besides assisting him in maintaining his near perfect swing, watching the videos helps reinforce the kind of pitches Gwynn can expect from each pitcher.[8]

But Tony goes beyond keeping and watching videos of his bat-ting. Each day when it is time for the Padres to take batting practice, do you know who is the first person in the batting cage working on his hitting? It's Tony Gwynn.[9] You see, Tony under-stands that even if you are one of the best hitters in baseball, you cannot "cram" and stay on top of your game for long. Even for one as highly talented as himself, Tony Gwynn knows that the "Law of the Farm" applies.

Finally, the syllabus. As you sit in the worship service this morning, I want you to imagine for the next few moments that this sanctuary is a classroom and this is the first class meeting of the semester (similar to today being the first Sunday after school has started back or being the first Sunday of a new church year). Now I want you to imagine that you have come on the first day of class along with most all of the other students who have registered for the class. Students tend to show up for the initial class meeting because they want to find out the requirements of the course. They may not always come to class (and some of them may not show up again for a long time), but generally students will come on the first day to get the syllabus—to find out what's expected.

So you have come for this first class meeting. The professor (the Master Instructor if you will) is not present, although you can somehow almost sense his presence. But the professor has sent his graduate assistant to hand out the syllabus and talk to the class about course requirements and other introductory matters. Further imagine, if you will (and this may stretch your imagination somewhat), that I have been asked to be the graduate assistant.

Now imagine that the syllabus that I am going to give to the class is really something that is given out every week (Sunday) of the world when we assemble here. It's on the front of the bulletin. It's the mission statement of this church. It goes as follows:

Calvary Baptist Church is a Christ-centered, caring church family in the center of our community. Our mission is to love God and each other, and to share with others the Good News of Jesus Christ as we worship, teach, serve, and nurture spiritual growth.

That's our mission. That's your syllabus. Now that I've "handed out" the syllabus, let me offer you some suggestions that—if followed—should help you complete this course in a satisfactory manner:

(1) *Pay attention to the syllabus.* Remember, it contains the purpose (mission) of this course. Periodically re-read the syllabus so that you will be reminded why this course is in the curriculum.

(2) *Attend class regularly.* You are responsible for knowing what happens in class whether you are present or not. You never know what you might miss if you are not here: an African children's choir singing, a homeless person wandering in off the street needing help, a young person or adult making his/her public profession of faith in Jesus Christ, a college student participating in the service.

(3) *Keep up with daily assignments.* Don't wait until the end of the semester (church year) and then try to "cram" everything. You'll still understand some of what you need to know by "cramming," but not nearly as much as if you are present and keep up with your assignments each day.

(4) *Read the textbook.* Don't try to get along by just relying on what others say the textbook (Bible) says. Read it and interpret it for yourself. In order to gain the full benefits of this course, you need to read the text. Resolve not to come to class without "cracking" the textbook (a book that we talk about so much yet actually is read so little).

(5) *Communicate with your instructor.* Remember, he is a Master Professor who desires to know each of his students. Don't think he's too busy to talk with you. He's not. Don't just sit back and pretend that you know it all or that everything is going well if that is not the case. If you are in trouble, tell him. If you've got a problem, let him know. It's called communication. (It's called prayer.)

(6) *Apply what you learn when you are outside the classroom.* The content of this course is very pragmatic by design. It is intended to help you with life, not just with taking a class and getting a degree. Share what you learn with others. You might even want to encourage them to sign up for this course, too.

(7) *Be ready for the tests.* Notice that the syllabus does not say that test number one will be October 3, and the second test will be November 2, and the final exam will be the first week in December. The tests for this course may come at any time and at any place. (You'll be tested on the campus and in the dorm room and at social gatherings. You'll be tested in the community and at

various places of business. You'll even be tested in the privacy of your home when you think no one except your family is watching.) Remember that in this course you are going to be tested all the time.

As your graduate assistant (and as a fellow student), let me offer each of you best wishes as another "semester" (church year) gets underway. We who are here today really do have an opportunity to learn from and to "grow in the knowledge of" our Master Instructor. We have the opportunity to join this Master Teacher in the work that he is doing in our world.

We have been given our assignment. We know our mission. We've got the syllabus. But we cannot complete the course to our fullest potential if we revert to "cramming." We won't be all that successful if we are content just to show up every once in a while. The challenge of our Teacher to all of his students/disciples is timeless and constant: "If any want to become my followers let them deny themselves and take up their cross *daily* and follow me" (Luke 9:23).

I hope that you have a good semester, and I trust that our church will have a productive year. I hope that we will keep our eyes focused upon the Master Instructor, Jesus Christ, who calls upon each of us to give him our best.

And I hope that we will remember some of the principles that we have discussed on this "opening" day. For in so many areas of life—including our faith and this course called Christianity— "cramming" will not produce the most fruitful results in the long run. The "Agriculture of the Spirit" of Galatians 6:7-10 is forever relevant. The "Law of the Farm" applies.

Notes

[1] This sermon was first delivered on "University Day" at Calvary Baptist Church in Lexington, Kentucky—the first Sunday of the fall semester when many students from the University of Kentucky, Transylvania University, and Georgetown College attend worship services for the first time or return to the church from summer vacations.

[2] Stephen R. Covey, A. Roger Merrill, and Rebecca R. Merrill, *First Things First* (New York: Simon & Schuster, 1994) 55.

[3] The concept of the "Law of the Farm" is from Covey, 54-56.

[4] Raymond Stamm, "The Epistle to the Galatians," *The Interpreter's Bible* (New York: Abingdon Press, 1953) 10: 579-85.

[5] Covey, 54.

[6] Oscar Green, *Daily Guideposts 1993* (Carmel NY: Guideposts, 1992) 233.

[7] Hal Bodley, "Gwynn's Son, Dad Have Role in Chase," *USA Today*, Monday, July 25, 1994, 3C.

[8] Ibid.

[9] Ibid.

The Tale the Scars Tell

Galatians 6:11–18

Johnny F. McKinney

From now on, let no one make trouble for me; for I carry the marks of Jesus branded on my body. Galatians 6:17

Several years ago I was in Nashville, Tennessee, for a committee meeting when news of a terrible crime was reported in the local newspaper. A family from Texas was visiting in Nashville. A knock came at their motel door, and the stranger outside yelled, "I've run into your car." The father impulsively opened the door, only to be faced by a hostile intruder. The father and mother were locked in the bathroom, their daughter was raped, and their money stolen. The perpetrator was captured within a matter of hours, in part due to an unusual mark, a tattoo, on his body—a mark of infamy and shame, a badge of dishonor.

The ancient Jewish historian, Josephus, wrote of another type of mark or scar. Julius Caesar had followed the Roman general, Pompey, into Egypt. The Egyptian ruler captured Pompey and had him beheaded. Caesar promptly declared war on Egypt and won, with the help of Antipater, father of Herod the Great. Later, Antipater was accused of disloyalty against Caesar. In his defense, Antipater removed his robe revealing the marks of battle upon his body and declared: "These scars were gained fighting the battles of Caesar." They were marks of courage and loyalty.

When Paul defended himself against his opponents in Galatia, he offered as evidence the "marks of Jesus branded on my body."

Paul's opponents accused him of not preaching the whole gospel, of being a people pleaser, and of being less than a legitimate apostle (see 1:6ff). Throughout the letter of Galatians Paul had defended his gospel and his calling as an apostle. Now that he had finished with his verbal arguments, Paul called into evidence the indisputable facts, "the marks of Jesus" branded upon his body. His loyalty and commitment to Christ should have been without question.

The figure of speech Paul chose is an interesting one. Behind it is the Greek word from which our English word "stigma" comes. The word was used in Paul's day to describe brand marks upon domestic animals, slaves, criminals, soldiers, and devotees to certain religious cults. It implied ownership, servitude, and protection. Moffatt attempted to get at the meaning of the phrase when he rendered it, "For I bear branded on my body the owner's stamp of the Lord Jesus."

But what kind of identifying mark was Paul talking about? Did he actually have the name of Jesus tattooed upon his body? Not likely.

Paul was likely talking about the physical marks and scars upon his body that resulted from his unflinching devotion and service to Jesus Christ. He used similar language when he addressed the church at Corinth.

> We are hard pressed on every side, but not crushed; perplexed, but not in despair; persecuted, but not abandoned; struck down, but not destroyed. We always carry around in our body the death of Jesus, so that the life of Jesus may also be revealed in our body. (2 Cor 4:8f)

These marks on Paul stood in contrast to the mark of circumcision, of which his opponents boasted. Paul's commitment to Christ had been no small matter. It had been costly. If we were to say to Paul, "Tell us about those scars on your head, and those nasty marks on your back," he no doubt would remember many of the episodes. There was the stoning, the floggings, the shipwrecks, the beatings, the harsh exposure to the elements, and the wear and tear of his missionary travels (see 2 Cor 6:4-10; 11:23ff). If those scars could talk, they would tell quite a story—a story of allegiance to the cause of Christ. Those were not credentials that could be hung on a wall, but rather had been branded on the flesh in the midst of a daily routine of following Christ. Paul exhorted his troublemakers to "cease and desist"; his calling and commitment were clear.

All of this raises an interesting question for me. I wonder, are there any marks of Jesus upon my life? I am not referring to physical scars, such as those Paul could display. What about other distinguishing features? Are there things about my existence that are only attributable to the presence of Jesus in my life?

Maxie Dunnam offers a meditation upon this thought and this passage:

> . . . and Paul—He claimed it
> "I bear the marks of Jesus branded on my body";
> But what about me?
> What is my stigmata?
> At least this Lord—
> That I will be a sign of your presence to others,
> Your love through my love
> Your forgiveness through my forgiveness,
> Your acceptance through my acceptance;
> That I will give unstintingly
> In hospitality to others;
> That my heart will be a place of welcome,
> Open to every pilgrim or stranger
> Who seeks a listening ear or an embrace of acceptance
> That I will enter into the pain and joy
> The tears and laughter of others so completely
> I will be one with them
> And because I am one with you
> That they will receive you, O Christ from me.[1]

I believe our lives, individually and collectively, should bear marks of our relationship to Christ. The old question may seem trite to many, but it contains a great deal of truth: "If they were to put you on trial for being a Christian, would there be enough evidence to find you guilty?"

What are some of those things that demonstrate our relationship with Jesus? I offer three proposals. In part, they are something of a summary of Paul's message to the Galatians.

I.

One distinguishing mark upon our lives should be that of Conversion. What really marked Paul, beyond the physical scars, was the cross of Christ. Paul was a new person. The cross is not only something that happened to Christ, it is something that happens to his followers as well. The cross becomes a way of life. Paul emphatically declared:

> May I never boast of anything except the cross of our Lord Jesus Christ, by which the world has been crucified to me, and I to the world. For neither circumcision nor uncircumcision is anything; but a new creation is everything. (Gal 6:14-15)

Paul was not the same person he was prior to his encounter with Christ. As he affirmed to the church at Corinth, "So if anyone is in Christ, there is a new creation: everything old has passed away; see, everything has become new!" (2 Cor 5:17) What mattered to Paul was this transforming relationship to Jesus Christ, not following external niceties of law and ritual. We are properly related to God on the basis of faith; not by works of the law!

Paul bore more than physical marks upon his body! He demonstrated this new way of life:

> I have been crucified with Christ; and it is no longer I who live, but it is Christ who lives in me. And the life I now live in the flesh I live by faith in the Son of God, who loved me and gave himself for me. (Gal 2:19b-20)

Do we bear those signs of conversion? Is it clear that we are new persons in Christ? Leo Tolstoy expressed it well when he wrote, "When I came to believe in Christ's teaching, I ceased desiring what I had wished for before. The direction of my life, my desires, became different. What was good and bad changed places."

In a similar vein, George Will has observed that

> Christianity is a religion of unadjusted people whose obligation is to adjust to something that transcends the culture of the day, any day. We are called to adjust our lives to the Lordship of God in Jesus Christ, and that has always been revolutionary.[2]

Our baptismal experience identifies us as marked people—those who have died to self in order to live for Christ. We take on something of his life. It is one of the remarkable claims of the New Testament that human character can change. We don't have to stay the way we are! We begin to reap a harvest of the fruit of the Spirit: love, joy, peace, patience, kindness, generosity, faithfulness, gentleness, and self-control (see Gal 5:22f). We take on the character of Christ. His life becomes reflected in our own.

There are many intriguing stories that circulate around the life and career of Alexander the Great. I am told that when Alexander the Great ruled, he made it his policy to hear any appeal made to him from his soldiers. One day a young soldier was brought before Alexander for trial. The young man wore the tunic of Alexander's army. "With what is he charged?" asked Alexander, who held authority in all matters. There would be no appeal of his verdict. "He is charged with cowardice in battle," answered the prosecutor.

A great hush fell over the crowd gathered in the judgment hall. They knew Alexander as a general who expected his men to be gallant since he, himself, did not push his soldiers but led them into the thick of battle. Alexander looked at the young soldier who was a mere youth, fair haired and still too young to shave. The angry scowl on his face slowly changed into an understanding smile, "What is your name, soldier?" "Worthy King," responded the youth, "my name is as yours—Alexander."

Anger came back into Alexander's face, and he leaped to his feet. Alexander grabbed the soldier's tunic. "Young soldier," he said with great control, "either change your name, or change your behavior."

Does our behavior reflect our relationship to Christ, whose name we bear? Is the mark of conversion upon us?

II.

A second distinguishing mark upon us should be that of Calling. Paul was not only a new person in Christ, he also lived with a new compulsion. He was marked by a sense of commission and calling. Much of the letter of Galatians is a defense of his calling. Paul was not interested in making a good showing in the flesh, or in avoiding persecution because of his commitment to Christ (see 1:10-12;5:12f). His calling did not originate with a human source, but with Jesus Christ (see 1:1). Paul not only experienced conversion in his encounter with Jesus, he also received a calling to be about the work of Christ in the world.

> I am a debtor both to Greeks and to barbarians, both to the wise and to the foolish—hence my eagerness to proclaim the gospel to you also who are in Rome. For I am not ashamed of the gospel; it is the power of God for salvation to everyone who has faith, to the Jew first and also to the Greek. (Rom 1:14-16)

Paul's life would now be lived out under divine compulsion. He would be an instrument in the hands of God, carrying the good news of this gospel to the outer limits of his world.

God's calling comes to every Christian. It is not reserved for the Paul's of this world; nor is it limited to a few select Christians or ministers. All believers are called to be a part of God's team, to share his mission in the world. We are privileged not only to share God's life as it is revealed in Christ, we are also privileged to share that life with others. Christianity is not a private matter to be hoarded. We are called upon to engage our world with the transforming message and ministry of Jesus Christ.

German pastor and martyr Dietrich Bonhoeffer knew something about that calling. He challenged us when he wrote:

> The call of Christ . . . sets the Christian in the middle of the daily arena against sin and the devil. . . . Every day . . . he must suffer anew for Jesus Christ's sake. The wounds and scars he receives in the fray are living tokens of this participation in the cross of Christ.[3]

Hard and fast distinctions between laity and clergy are out of place. Every Christian is equipped by the Holy Spirit to fulfill his or her calling. God has a purpose for all our lives. We have experienced freedom in Christ, not to do as we please, but to love and to become servants to one another and to a hurting world.

The late Owen Cooper, distinguished Christian businessperson from Yazoo City, Mississippi, and a former president of the Southern Baptist Convention, argued for this sense of calling for all Christians:

> I am not a layman, I am not an amateur, I am not a novice, I am not a second class citizen in the Kingdom of God, and I do not want to be called by any of these names according to the current practice and meaning of these names among Southern Baptists. Call me a sinner, call me a saved sinner, call me a slave, call me a servant, call me a minister, call me a co-laborer, call me a yokefellow, call me a sojourner, call me a follower of the way, call me a child of God, call me a member of the "laos" (people of God), call me a saint, or call me by any other biblical term but do not call me a non-biblical term.[4]

It is obvious that Cooper was turned on by the biblical notion of calling. We cannot hire someone else to fulfill our calling. Christianity is not a spectator sport. Is this mark of Jesus upon our lives? Are we participating in the mission of God in the world?

III.

A third distinguishing mark upon our lives is that of Community. As followers of Christ, people marked by him, we experience not only conversion and calling, but also a new place of belonging. We are a part of a new community—a transformed and transforming body. Paul called the church the "Israel of God" (6:16); in Christ we are "Abraham's offspring, heirs according to the promise" (3:29). This new relationship is not on the basis of circumcision or keeping the law, but rather is granted by the Spirit and made possible in Christ.

This new community is characterized by freedom (5:1, 13) and new life in the spirit (5:16f). Old boundaries are demolished and barriers that divide the human family are to be done away with. As Paul declared: "There is no longer Jew or Greek, there is no longer slave or free, there is no longer male and female; for all of you are one in Christ Jesus" (3:28).

Shortly after the devastation of the First World War, Quakers brought relief to the impoverished people of Poland. They distributed food and clothing, along with other relief measures. One of the Quaker relief workers contracted typhus and quickly died. There were only Roman Catholic cemeteries in the tiny Polish village, and church law forbade burying anyone not of that faith in consecrated ground. So the Quakers buried their friend in a grave just outside the Catholic cemetery. The next morning, however, there was a surprise. During the night the villagers had moved the fence so that the cemetery now included the grave of the Quaker relief worker.[5]

These fence movers understood the nature of the gospel and Christian community. They redrew the boundaries of community.

For Paul, being Jewish and male, it would have been no easy task to drop traditional barriers. He realized, however, in Christ they must come down. There is no place in this new community we call the church for divisions based on gender, ethnic back-

ground, or social status for "all of you are one in Christ." There is
no room for boasting in regard to any advantage, "except the cross
of our Lord Jesus Christ" (6:14).

Do we carry the "brand marks" of Jesus upon us? Is it obvious
to the world that Jesus is our Lord—obvious because of our conversion, our calling, and our community? Is there enough evidence
against us to cause a "guilty" verdict to be rendered if we were put
on trial for being a Christian?

The words of Isaac Watts form a fitting challenge and
benediction:

> When I survey the wondrous cross,
> Where the young Prince of glory died,
> My richest gain I count but loss,
> And pour contempt on all my pride.
>
> Forbid it, Lord, that I should boast
> Save in the death of Christ, my God;
> All the vain things that charm me most,
> I sacrifice them to his blood.
>
> See from his head, his hands, his feet,
> Sorrow and love flow mingled down;
> Did e'er such love and sorrow meet,
> Or thorns compose so rich a crown?
>
> Were the whole realm of nature mine,
> That were a present far too small;
> Love so amazing, so divine,
> Demands my soul, my life, my all.[6]

Notes

[1]Maxie Dunnam, *The Communicator's Commentary* (Waco TX: Word Books, 1982) 134.

[2]*ID FORUM* (Winslow AR: AA Publishing, undated) 6.

[3]Dietrich Bonhoeffer, *The Cost of Discipleship* (New York: Macmillan Company, 1959) 79.

[4]I have not been able to locate the speech in which Mr. Cooper originally offered these lines.

[5]As retold by Donald E. Messer, *A Conspiracy of Goodness,* "Contemporary Images of Christian Mission," (Nashville: Abingdon Press, 1992) 127.

[6]Isaac Watts, "When I Survey the Wondrous Cross," 1707.

Biographical Notes

Robert G. Baker is pastor of Calvary Baptist Church, Lexington, Kentucky. He is a graduate of Georgetown College, where he has also been the chair of the board of trustees, and of the Southern Baptist Theological Seminary (M.Div., Ph.D.), where he has been an instructor in Old Testament. His other pastorates have been in Kentucky.

Charles B. Bugg is pastor of Providence Baptist Church in Charlotte, North Carolina. For four years he was the Carl E. Bates Professor of Preaching at Southern Baptist Theological Seminary, Louisville, Kentucky. Other pastorates include First Baptist Church, Augusta, Georgia, and First Baptist Church, Deland, Florida. He is a graduate of Stetson University and the Southern Baptist Theological Seminary (M.Div., Ph.D.) and has done additional study at Princeton Theological Seminary and the Candler School of Theology, Emory University.

Vaughn CroweTipton is campus life coordinator at the Methodist Children's Home, Macon, Georgia. He is also a New Testament Ph.D. student at Baylor University. A graduate of Mississippi College and the Southern Baptist Theological Seminary (M.Div.), he has served churches in Mississippi, Kentucky, and Texas.

Vernon E. Davis is vice president for academic affairs and professor of Christian theology at Midwestern Baptist Theological Seminary. He is a graduate of Baylor University and Southwestern Baptist Theological Seminary (B.D., Th.D.). For twelve years he was pastor of First Baptist Church, Alexandria, Virginia. In Texas he served several churches and was the Baptist Student Union director at Rice University.

Mark E. Hopper is pastor of First Baptist Church, Frankfort, Kentucky. He is a graduate of Oklahoma Baptist University and the Southern Baptist Theological Seminary (M.Div., Ph.D.). He has been the pastor of other Kentucky churches and has taught New Testament and Greek at Southern Seminary.

Gregory L. Hunt is senior minister of Holmeswood Baptist Church in Kansas City, Missouri. A graduate of Baylor University and the Southern Baptist Theological Seminary (M.Div., Ph.D), he has served churches in Kentucky and Louisiana. A contributor to other publications, he included one of his sermons in Smyth & Helwys' *Amidst Babel, Speak the Truth.*

Thomas R. McKibbens, Jr., is senior minister of First Baptist Church in Newton, Massachusetts, and has served other churches in Massachusetts, Virginia, and Kentucky. He was associate professor of preaching at Southeastern Baptist Theological Seminary and a visiting professor of preaching at the Southern Baptist Theological Seminary and Harvard Divinity School. He is the author of *The Forgotten Heritage: A Lineage of Great Baptist Preaching* (Mercer University Press).

Johnny F. McKinney is pastor of Boulevard Baptist Church, Anderson, South Carolina. He has served other churches in South Carolina, Tennessee, and Kentucky and holds degrees from Milligan College and Southern Baptist Theological Seminary (M.Div., D.Min.). He has also taught at Gardner-Webb College and has contributed sermons previously to the Kerygma and Church series.

C. Alan Melton is pastor of Orange Baptist Church, Orange, Virginia. He is a graduate of the University of Georgia and Southern Baptist Theological Seminary (M.Div., D.Min.). A licensed pastoral counselor, he has also participated in the Virginia Institute of Pastoral Care pastoral counseling training program. He has served churches in North Carolina, Kentucky, and Virginia.

Scott Nash is senior vice president, book division, Smyth & Helwys Publishing, Inc.; managing editor for Mercer University Press; and adjunct associate professor of Christianity at Mercer University. A graduate of Centre College and the Southern Baptist Theological Seminary (M.Div., Ph.D.), he was the Barney Averitt chair of Religion and chair of the division of Religious and Philosophical Studies at Brewton-Parker College. He has been the pastor of churches in Kentucky and Georgia.

Kate Penfield is minister of the First Baptist Church in America, Providence, Rhode Island. She is a graduate of the State University of New York at Albany, University of Cincinnati (M.Ed.), and Andover-Newton Theological School (M.Div.). Denominational service in the American Baptist Churches USA includes editing the denominational journal, *The Minister*, and filling the office of vice-president.

John B. Polhill is professor of New Testament studies and director of graduate studies at the Southern Baptist Theological Seminary, from which he earned the M.Div. and Ph.D. degrees. Also a graduate of the University of Richmond, he has done post-doctoral study at Princeton Theological Seminary and the University of California at Berkeley. His book on the Acts of the Apostles appears in the New American Commentary series.

Howard W. Roberts has held pastorates in Maryland, Georgia, and Kentucky, and is presently at First Baptist Church, Auburn, Alabama. A graduate of Georgetown College and the Southern Baptist Theological Seminary (M.Div., D.Min.), he has contributed sermons and articles to several periodicals and has published several books, including *Learning to Pray, The Lasting Words of Jesus, Redemptive Responses of Jesus,* and *Approaching the Third Millennium* and *Sins That Crucify* (published by Smyth & Helwys).

Marion L. Soards is professor of New Testament studies at the Louisville Presbyterian Seminary. He is a graduate of Furman University, the Southern Baptist Theological Seminary (M.Div.), Union Theological Seminary in New York City (M.Phil., S.T.M., Ph.D.), and Ludwig-Maximillans University, Munich, Germany (U.D.G.Z.). He has also taught at Louisiana State University and United Theological Seminary. In 1991–1992 he was guest professor in Münster, Germany, under the auspices of Westfälische Wilhelms-Universität. He is the author of more than forty articles and seventeen books.

Ronda Stewart-Wilcox is minister of education at May Memorial Baptist Church, Powhatan, Virginia. She is a graduate of Texas Tech University, Baylor University (M.A.), and the Southern Baptist Theological Seminary (M.Div.). She has served other churches in Kentucky and is currently the treasurer for the board of Southern Baptist Women in Ministry.

W. Clyde Tilley teaches at Lane College in Jackson, Tennessee. Previously, he taught at Union University. He is a graduate of Carson-Newman College, Memphis State University (M.A.), and the Southern Baptist Theological Seminary (M.Div., Ph.D.). His book on the Sermon on the Mount, *The Surpassing Righteousness*, was published by Smyth & Helwys.

William L. Turner is pastor of South Main Baptist Church, Houston, Texas. A graduate of Samford University, the Southern Baptist Theological Seminary (M.Div., Th.M.), and Lexington Theological Seminary (D.Min.), he has served churches in Kentucky. Smyth & Helwys published his book, *The Struggle to Believe*.